Praise for *Work Is Fun*

"Steve's spot on. Enjoying work isn't about salary, perks, or status—it's about being truly invested in what you're doing. We've seen this time and again as we help our clients implement EOS. When people are having fun at work, it leads to sustained engagement and productivity."

—Gino Wickman, Author, *Traction* and *Shine*, and Creator, EOS®

"Having watched King of Pops grow, I've seen firsthand how fun is baked into everything they do. *Work Is Fun* is a powerful reminder that the best work is meaningful, and even fun."

—Kat Cole, CEO, AG1

"Steve Carse is the consummate entrepreneur's entrepreneur, with a never-ending thirst for learning and experimentation. Steve has started a number of businesses under the Rainbow Umbrella brands, the most famous of which is King of Pops. In his book *Work Is Fun*, Steve takes the reader through an incredible journey of ups and downs, zigs and zags, and arrives at an inspiring conclusion: Work is fun. Work is creativity. Work is self-expression. And, in one of the most important distinctions, work is something we should enjoy doing. Steve outlines his vision and opinion on this like only a successful entrepreneur can."

—David Cummings, CEO, Atlanta Ventures

"A powerful tale of turning pain into purpose, and crafting the life you truly want."

—Andrew Wilkinson, Cofounder, Tiny, and Author, *Never Enough*

"Entrepreneur Steven Carse is self-aware and sophisticated. He mixes his joy of being a business owner with his insights as a man of bold perspectives in *Work Is Fun*, his first book about making ice pops. This flavor maven is a force of nature, reminding us to *enjoy* work—which eases stress and tension—a proven strategy for living a longer and fulfilling life. So I recommend this read not only for the business hacks but also as an introduction to his treats for your palate!"

—Lisa Borders, Multisector Business Strategist and
Operator, and former President, WNBA

"King of Pops is one of my favorite small business stories I have ever experienced. I have been a fan of the product and the leader since day one. This book reveals the secrets to why I love their brand. If you are in the grind and need a fresh perspective on your work, I 100% recommend this book to bring fun back to work!"

—Jeff Shinabarger, Founder, Plywood People, and
Host, *The Social Impact Leader Podcast*

WORK IS FUN

WORK IS FUN

Seven Ways a Successful
Ice Pop Company Makes Work
Meaningful and How You Can Too

STEVE CARSE

Matt Holt Books
An Imprint of BenBella Books, Inc.
Dallas, TX

Matt Holt is an imprint of BenBella Books, Inc.
8080 N. Central Expressway
Suite 1700
Dallas, TX 75206
benbellabooks.com
Send feedback to feedback@benbellabooks.com

BenBella and *Matt Holt* are federally registered trademarks.

Printed in the United States of America
10 9 8 7 6 5 4 3 2 1

Library of Congress Control Number: 2024043090
ISBN 9781637746257 (hardcover)
ISBN 9781637746264 (electronic)

Editing by Katie Dickman
Copyediting by Evan Herrington
Proofreading by Karen Wise and Cheryl Beacham
Text design and composition by PerfecType, Nashville, TN
Cover design by Dani Does Design
Printed by Sheridan MI

*To Leigh & Will—may your nine-to-fives
and five-to-nines both bring you joy.*

CONTENTS

AN ODE TO ICE POPS, A SHORT FOREWORD, AND A SALUTE TO THE SHARED BELIEF THAT WORK SURE CAN BE FUN

Ari Weinzweig

What you're holding in your hands is, I'm pretty confident, the only book in existence that brings together the beauty of ice pops and positive business; connects stories of successfully extracting lost Frisbees from disc golf ponds with excellence in entrepreneurship; and that merges the successful selling of one-of-a-kind, custom-created ice pop flavors with fun and finding purpose.

I loved reading it.

If you didn't put it down after that first sentence, I'm pretty sure you will too. If you do read *Work Is Fun*, you will learn, you'll laugh, you'll relate, and, as per its title, you will almost certainly have fun in the process.

We've been working at Zingerman's for a little longer than Steve Carse has been alive, and I've long since lost track of how many thousands of business books I've read over the years, but even with all that background as lead-up, I still learned a lot from this book. If you're open to a series of new, down-to-earth approaches to attaining excellence, I'm confident you will as well. And seriously, other than determined curmudgeons, superserious cynics, and a handful of corporate oligarchs who have so much money they no longer go into the office . . . well, seriously, who wouldn't want to read a book called *Work Is Fun*?

Work Is Fun will, as per its subtitle, generously share with you *Seven Ways a Successful Ice Pop Company Makes Work Meaningful and How You Can Too*. In the array of stories beneath the subtitle, aside from the seven ways, *Work Is Fun* also includes intriguing tales of postcollege existential crises; adrenaline-evoking emergencies in which the clock is ticking while artisan ice pops are melting in the summer heat of south Georgia; and life lessons learned from much-loved dogs, all of which are woven into a really well-written and fun-to-read business book.

It's been over 42 years now since my business partner Paul Saginaw and I first opened Zingerman's Delicatessen in Ann Arbor, Michigan. We started out with just the two of us and a couple of employees, all working in a small 1,300-square-foot space, with 29 seats, 25 sandwiches, and a whole lotta help from friends and family. All these years later, our collaboratively run, quality-focused, and collectively owned Zingerman's Community of Businesses includes a dozen different Zingerman's businesses (each with its own specialty—there's still, as is our wont, only one Deli) here in the Ann Arbor area with a total staff of over 700 and cumulative sales of something like $80,000,000.

So much of what we've been able to accomplish over the years is thanks to learnings we gathered and gleaned from others who had gone before us and who were willing to then generously share their wisdom with the world. One of our many "teachers" was Paul Hawken. In his 1987 book *Growing a Business*, Hawken shares the story of one of his early business successes. You may already know a bit about Smith and Hawken. Started in 1979, it was an innovative mail-order company that made its way in the world by reworking and selling hand-crafted, traditionally made, artisan garden tools in a marketplace that had moved more and more toward cheap, mass-produced alternatives. I wasn't a gardener, but I loved the way Smith and Hawken seemed to work. Even though I didn't need what they were selling, it made me *want* to get into gardening just so I'd have a reason to partake in what they were purveying. In his book, Paul Hawken explained the company's success this way: "Smith and Hawken grew because it had its roots in a sense of what was lost . . . What had been lost was still needed."

Hawken goes on to expand and extrapolate from his own experience his belief that products that were once widely loved but have been lost, or lost their quality and integrity, will almost always be in demand. It's just that no one realizes that that demand is there. As Hawken writes, one of the best ways to make a great business, then, is to find one of those products and put it back into the marketplace. The world, he makes clear, will have been waiting for you to get to work. When you do, as Hawken has it, you will quickly be very busy! This is, in fact, what we have done here at Zingerman's with everything from corned beef to artisan candy bars, really great rye bread to fried chicken, cream cheese to exceptionally good ginger cookies. We have successfully made what was old new again at a quality level that was no longer found anywhere around us.

Steve and the crew at King of Pops have demonstrated the veracity of Paul Hawken's theory by doing much the same thing in south Georgia with ice pops as we've been able to do here with pastrami. While supermarkets and convenience stores have always sold Popsicles, the sort of old-school, far more flavorful, artisan-inspired offerings that Paul Hawken is suggesting were nowhere to be found. King of Pops has successfully changed all that, to the tune of annual sales of $10 million. As Paul Hawken put it poetically, it turns out "what had been lost was still needed." And as King of Pops has proven, also still eagerly and joyfully awaited!

With all that in mind, the book you hold in your hands is a happy and superhelpful walk through the world that Steve, his brother Nick, and the whole crew at King of Pops have created over 15 years of pop making. In *Work Is Fun*, Steve shares a whole range of lessons that can help us lead more rewarding lives, make our work a whole lot more rewarding, and turn what we do for a living into something that makes creativity, caring, and keeping "cool" into an uplifting, joyful, and joy-filled daily routine.

One of the best parts of our work here at Zingerman's is, I believe, that we have the opportunity—through ZingTrain, our training business, and through the books and pamphlets I write—to do for other values-aligned businesspeople what Paul Hawken did nearly 40 years ago for us here at Zingerman's. To help demonstrate that one can be successful in business without doing bad things; that our organizations can help make the world a better place; that, as we often say here, one can do business differently; and that we can have fun while we're working our collective butts off to make it happen. King of Pops, I'm happy to say, fits all those bills. I don't know Paul Hawken personally, but I imagine he would be happy to know that his teaching helped us to make the Zingerman's Community of Businesses what it is today. I do, though, know Steve Carse, and I can say with certainty that I am humbled and honored to see so clearly that we have helped him on his path. I feel confident that somewhere around 2050, some other new business owner, unconsciously following a path similar to the one that has made both Zingerman's and King of Pops what they are today, will be reading *Work Is Fun*. In it, I'm confident, they will find much of the same sort of inspiration I got from Paul Hawken so many decades ago.

Read up, learn a lot, stay cool, work hard, make a difference, and, absolutely, have some good fun while you're doing it.

INTRODUCTION

The back of one of my two-for-one Men's Wearhouse dress shirts was sticking to the driver's seat as I slowly rolled down the interstate on my commute back into the city.

It was a Friday, I was 25 years old, and I was eager to get my weekend started.

My driver's side window had been busted out for the second time in three months, so even on full blast, the AC could not keep up with the sticky midsummer heat rising from the asphalt.

It was supposed to be a reverse commute. The office I worked out of was in the suburbs, but I refused to live nearby as I was focused on maximizing my nonworking hours. The city, my friends, girls, pretty much everything I wanted other than my job were in town.

The guy who broke into my car had stolen my gym bag and my radio, so I was stuck listening to the shockingly loud murmur of neighboring engines.

As I looked around, the faces of my fellow commuters seemed closer than ever. Their expressions were tinged with tension and rage. It was supposed to be a joyous time—the work week had concluded and we had been set free—only to find ourselves drowning in a sea of brake lights.

I felt simultaneously frustrated and connected with the strangers rolling along next to me. We had just wasted 40 hours of our lives toiling away at who knows what so someone who probably already had more money than they could ever spend could have a little bit more.

I motioned for a lady to merge in front of me, then surprised myself by letting out a yell.

Nobody saw me.

Nobody heard me.

But unfortunately, it didn't make me feel any better.

I imagined myself making this drive for 40 more years, and it made me sad.

Have you ever had this feeling?

Have you ever felt like you were wasting away the best years of your life doing something that had no point?

My job at the time wasn't so bad. I had my own cubicle decorated with ironic posters and bobbleheads, a boss who was nice and took me to get a beer every once in a while, and relatively little stress.

But time dragged by. I would catch myself checking the clock every couple of minutes, looking forward to the end of the day.

I had worked so hard to get to this point in my life, but now it felt like I was going to be stuck on rinse and repeat for my best years, spending most of my days doing something that provided a paycheck but little more.

Lucky for me, I didn't have that many of these commutes left.

I was about to be laid off, and with the fear of wasting my life away at another job that was "just OK" echoing inside of my head, I decided to start my own thing.

A year later, on a similarly hot summer day, I was once again sweating. This time, however, I was in a T-shirt, standing under a rainbow umbrella. Sweat was pouring down my face, but I couldn't stop smiling.

I'd spent all my savings, about $7,000, to bootstrap a tiny business called King of Pops, and things were going surprisingly well.

I was on a mission to introduce Atlanta to our take on the Popsicle. I was working more than ever, and if there was more time in the day, I would have happily worked even more.

When I went to bed each night, my mind was flooded with new ideas. I had to keep a notepad next to my bed to jot them down or else I couldn't fall asleep, fearing I'd forget some valuable insight.

My work as a whole felt meaningful.

Before starting, I had been working to enable the other parts of my life, and somehow now my work was enhancing every part of my life.

I'd later learn to call this new feeling "work-life blend," a more desirable and realistic option than the "work-life balance" touted on job postings from well-intentioned companies.

I had already trudged through the "work-life balance" idea at my last job, and while yes, it was balanced, the work part left me feeling empty. My nonwork hours had to be epic to justify the blah that took place from nine to five.

If you can't imagine loving your work, this book is for you.

If you find yourself living for the weekend, an amazing vacation, or retirement, you can do so much better.

And if you think you just need to wait until you get your extra degree, earn a promotion, or get another raise, I have some bad news—none of those things on their own will make your work more fun.

I didn't know it at the time, but it didn't take going out on my own to enjoy my work. I didn't need to legally own a company, but I did need to change how I thought about the work I was doing.

Work is fun when we're making things happen instead of letting things happen to us.

I love entrepreneurship, but starting your own business is nothing more than a career path. It doesn't guarantee fulfillment; it's just another place to work with a different compensation plan. In order to have fun at work, doing any type of work, it will have to take on a different meaning. You don't need to be an owner, but you will have to learn to take ownership. You will have to become invested in the outcomes, not just your inputs.

The day-to-day hustle will only feel meaningful if you have a clear picture of where you want to go and why you want to be there.

In the early days of King of Pops, my goal was selfish. Burned out from spreadsheets, I wanted something different. I wanted work to be fun. Parenthood wasn't even on the radar at this point, but I still wanted to have a good story to tell my grandkids one day. The goal wasn't grandiose, but it felt important.

I thought I might do it for a year or two and then go back to something more "normal," but I'm still at it, and it has shaped me into the person I am today.

I'll never forget the first time I experienced work this way. It was a 19-hour day—the first day our fledgling ice pop business faced having to be in two places at once. My brother Nick, who had a "real job" as a lawyer at the time, would be working the cart at Buddy's gas station, our original and only location at the time, and I would be taking the show on the road to a small festival 30 minutes south of Atlanta.

But before all that, we arrived at our shared kitchen as the sun was coming up. We were far from experts when it came to making pops, and we had a couple of hours of work to do to finish up our pop-making run from the night before. At this point, we were doing our packaging in the walk-in freezer to avoid ugly semi-melted pops as we wrapped them.

We hustled to carefully seal the pops in their wrappers, shivering and laughing at ourselves. We hand-sealed each one, packed up our carts, gathered the day's supplies, and loaded both carts into the truck.

I dropped my brother and his cart off at the gas station, wished him luck, and headed south for my event.

Our setup was easy, and I had everything in place before the festival started. As people streamed in, I was eager to sell them a pop and anxious for them to try it.

The event was called May Day, and it was in a planned community called Serenbe that has a sustainability and local farming focus. Little did I know that the upper-middle-class farm-loving young families would soon be some of my best customers. I was too busy selling pops that day to second-guess anything. My insecurities all but vanished as I found myself in a flow state.

Halfway through the day, I realized I was going to run out of pops. I was selling out of certain flavors, and as I crossed them off the board, people in line let out audible moans. I'd apologize each time and encourage them to try the next flavor.

The festival was set to end at 6 PM, but by 2 PM, I had sold my last pop. Ecstatic, I went to buy a celebratory beer and a pricey farm-to-table sandwich. I was in no rush as I proudly stacked the bills I'd crammed in my pockets, making sure the presidents' faces were all pointing the same way.

Before I could finish the counting or my sandwich, Nick called. He seemed panicked. "We're out of pops," he said, "and the customers who showed up but didn't get pops are following me back to the kitchen to buy whatever we've got left!"

I left the festival and rushed back to our kitchen. In a haze, we made pops late into the night and woke up the next morning to do it again. I didn't know it, but that day my life changed forever. My somewhat involuntary corporate exodus would lead me on a lifelong journey that would allow for my work time to be truly fun instead of an eight-hour block of drudgery bookended by some enjoyable moments.

Fifteen years later, some things have changed about the day-to-day of leading King of Pops, but the fun still hasn't worn off. I look forward to getting to work each day, and I leave earlier than I want to in order to get to the other parts of my life.

However, my work is far from done. Although I personally enjoy my work quite a bit, I know this is not the case for each member of the King of Pops team all the time. We owe it to them to do better.

We want more people to take ownership of their work lives and, if we can help it, have a good time.

This book is a journey through what I've learned when I'm having fun at work, and a reminder that it is worth it to help others feel that same connection to their work. The ideas are simple and applicable to individuals and organizations of any size.

Too often, the default conversation about work is negative. When someone asks, "How was work?" the answer is rarely better than "OK."

There are so many people searching for a better job, but a change of scenery on its own will not change how you feel about work.

I've talked to students who've taken a gap year and adults who've had the good fortune to take a sabbatical. Even when we take much-needed time away from work to try and recalibrate, we are often searching for answers out in the universe to magically make our work more meaningful.

The idea is pure, but the expectations are unrealistic.

There is this notion that we will become different people during these moments we take away from work. We put a huge amount of pressure on ourselves, and then when we are on our break that we've anticipated so much, we feel just about the same. The setting may be beautiful, and sleeping in feels nice, but a change in location alone won't answer life's more difficult questions. These breaks can certainly recharge your batteries, but they do little to uncover what might bring you fulfillment in your day-to-day work.

I was at a similar breaking point when I got laid off from my corporate gig and started King of Pops. I didn't yet understand it fully, but I knew I wanted more out of life.

Through that experience, I was introduced to people who worked differently. They moved through the world in a way that was unlike that of the adults I had observed growing up.

Many of these folks were entrepreneurs, but as I recognized and eventually began to live out a similar path, it became clear that the freedom they enjoyed had nothing to do with the type of work they did or the positions they held. Once I started to pay attention, I saw trends across industries and experience levels.

It is super common to have a sense that your work mostly happens to you. There is this false assumption that there is a much smarter, more qualified group of people pulling the strings and making things happen for everyone else somewhere behind the scenes.

For this reason, it's easy to think your job is a sure thing that you don't have much control over. I know I felt that way working at American International Group (AIG), the largest insurance company in the world. By all practical accounts, that job should have been a sure thing, yet I watched layoff after layoff happen before my eyes until it eventually happened to me.

When we feel this way, it's easy to have the mindset that we're just along for the ride. But if you're an idle passenger, you won't get to where you want to go.

To have meaningful work, you've got to take control of your journey. Work matters when you believe it matters. It's a nice benefit if others think it matters, too, but it is really up to you.

More than likely, where you are working right now can be more fulfilling. It can even be fun. In the pages to come, we'll go through the steps to make that happen.

By the end of this book, you may decide there truly are outside forces making your current job unhealthy, uninspiring, unfun, and ultimately undoable. You might decide to find different work, but this book is not about the search for something else to work on. It's about refining your approach to work—the thing we will spend so much of our time doing.

So often we are willing to put in massive energy to improve the nonwork aspects of our lives—to heal a relationship, to raise great children, to get in shape and be healthy—but we don't think to put in that same effort to improve our relationship to work.

Like anything worthwhile, turning your job into something you look forward to won't be easy, but once you start to put in the effort to reflect on your journey, you'll suddenly realize you're having fun.

IS FUN THAT IMPORTANT?

Sometimes when I talk about having fun at work, or when I mention companies that don't make an effort to make their work fun, people say, "Well, work isn't supposed to be enjoyable."

They think it's all about the grind, and that if you have fun people won't take you seriously or think you're professional enough. But I'm here to tell you: it is officially OK to have fun and get paid at the exact same time.

To repeat: when I talk about fun, I don't mean being silly or childish (although there's a time and place for that). I'm talking about feeling engaged and curious, maybe even playful about work in a way that makes it enjoyable, especially when you work with a team committed to the same goals.

You might think fun isn't important at work, but the research overwhelmingly disagrees. Fun fosters community, engagement, and happiness—all of which make work more rewarding for individuals and far more profitable for the business. A meta-analysis from Gallup in 2024* found that businesses in the top quartile for engaged employees were 18% more productive and 23% more profitable than those in the bottom quartile. Who wouldn't jump at a chance to be 23% more profitable *while* you're having fun?

WANT MORE FUN?

A good life, to me, feels like it is overflowing. My goal, every day, is to enjoy it as much as possible.

On a normal Monday, when I'm about to drop my daughter off at preschool, part of me wants to skip drop-off and head to the zoo or doughnut shop with her instead to spend more time together.

In much the same way, when I'm at work, as the evening approaches and I inevitably haven't finished everything I'd hoped to get to, part of me wants to stick around and get more done.

In both instances I'm having fun, and I want to extend the current moment. At the same time, I'm looking forward to the next thing. These are the days when everything is going right. Once your life feels this way, you have to maintain the discipline and perspective to move from one thing to the next, even though you'd be quite content to stay put. If you're able to leave yourself wanting more, you've got something fun to come back to.

---

* Jim Harter, "3 Key Insights into the Global Workplace," Gallup, June 12, 2024, www.gallup.com/workplace/645416/key-insights-global-workplace.aspx.

Oddly enough, the discipline to stop having fun in the moment can lead to more fun overall.

Imagine a zenned-out surfer with a perma-smile on a tropical beach somewhere. He's cool, calm, and content. Perfectly happy to wait out the day, enjoying whatever waves come his way. Except this particular surfer doesn't just surf. He also has a challenging, fun job and a home life that fills him up.

His energy is consistently positive as he moves through the different parts of his life. He looks forward to a full, engaging day at work, he looks forward to coming home in the evening, and he looks forward to going to bed, then waking up in the morning to do it all again.

That is how I want to feel.

To be clear, I think life outside of work is the priority, but I know that when I'm having fun at work, I'm more pleasant everywhere else.

For most people, work is the segment of their life they'd be happy to do without. However, if you're like me, and work isn't optional, you should take the time to figure out how to enjoy it.

If you want more fun in your work life, it's possible. Whether you're an entry-level analyst, a middle manager, or in the C-suite of a major company, the concepts in this book can transform your approach to work and leadership for you, your team, and your whole organization.

I've spent the last 15 years building a business and having more fun than I ever thought possible at work! While making money! While doing the things I genuinely needed to do to support myself and my family!

I want you to have more fun too. My hope is that this book can help you invest your life in work that matters, have more fun, and fill your life with more hours you're looking forward to living.

The next seven chapters outline the seven ways that I've found lead to more fun at work. There will be bad days when things break and don't go your way, but with a good-natured awareness of these concepts circling around in your brain, you'll minimize the bad days and maximize the fun.

Here are the big principles to making work more fun that we'll tackle in the following chapters:

- **Story**. Make sure you're writing a good one.
- **Patience**. Good things take time, and while money is an important part of work, you can't let it control your career decisions.
- **Ownership**. Where it comes from, how to find it for yourself, and how to cultivate it with those around you.
- **Pride**. You can't just turn it on, but once it's there, it changes how every little thing at work feels.
- **Play**. We've found that being silly is about far more than just a quick laugh.
- **Teamwork**. The people around you will make or break your experience.
- **Tension**. It's sad but true: even with everything listed above in perfect harmony, things will continue to frustrate you and work will still test you, but it will all be worth it.

For those who are skeptical that work can actually be fun, or at least fun for you, chapter 8 talks about the most common objections you might have to the ideas in this book.

Like anything, it's a process. Dramatic changes in how you operate are not required and might lead to decisions you regret, but a consistent, gentle reframing of how you look at your work will do wonders for you and everyone around you. It's your choice.

How you act on that choice can vary depending on your role at work—if you're an employee or if you're in charge. If you get stuck, each chapter ends with some more direct, practical thoughts for applying each principle, depending on where you are in your career—"When It's Up to You" and also "When It's Not Up to You."

Throughout our careers, we zig and zag between these two realities.

There are plenty of things at work that you may not have any control over. For example, if you work at a coffee shop and your shift starts at 5 AM, you don't have much control over when you need to show up.

However, when it comes to writing your own work story, you've got the final say. You'll navigate trade-offs, risks, and responsibilities, but at every turn, you're the lone author.

Your personal work story could be adventurous, humanitarian, educational, artistic, environmental, or health focused.

You could start your own thing, or it could be landing your dream job at an organization you love, making a name for yourself, and putting your unique stamp on history.

Finally, we'll wrap it all up with a big team huddle to make our workplaces (and lives!) more fun.

The time for fun is always right now. These are the good ol' days.

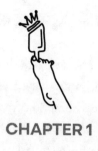

CHAPTER 1

Write an Epic Story

KING OF POPS BEGINNINGS

The idea for King of Pops started on a series of trips I took through Central America with my two brothers, Nick and Ashley. My oldest brother, Ashley, is an anthropologist, and throughout my college years and beyond, my default summer trip was to visit him in different parts of the world. When we're away from home, we allow ourselves to see the world a little differently.

We did our best to act like locals in the areas we visited, but when the three of us were traveling together, there was little we could do to hide the fact that we were tourists. Three blondish guys walking down the street together already kind of stick out in most parts of the world, but we were also each a full head taller than most of the locals, making it nearly impossible to blend in.

Tourists or not, we tried to absorb as much of the authentic culture in an area as we could. We avoided the backpacker hangouts, refused to dine at the chain restaurants we'd seen before, and did our best to avoid major tourist traps.

I lucked into a world-class set of older brothers. Ashley has always gone out of his way to encourage Nick and me to look beneath the surface and challenge the assumptions that we've learned growing up. He lined up activities for us, and we went on hikes and fishing trips and wandered through street markets. But the most memorable parts of the trip always came from something unplanned.

Without thinking much of it, we bought our first *paleta*, the Latin American version of the beloved Popsicle, killing time after missing a bus in Puerto Escondido, a fishing village with beautiful beaches in Mexico. I think I ate three in a row that afternoon while we were waiting.

From then on, we started to seek them out. We didn't have a travel agenda in place, and before we knew it, the search for the world's best *paleta* became the backdrop of our exploring.

These *paletas* were not just for kids. They had straightforward flavors, but they also had options for a more sophisticated palate. There were options with spicy peppers, flowers, herbs, corn, coffee, nuts, and every fruit you could ever imagine.

The weirder, the better. The more flavors we tried, the more excited we got.

We enjoyed them so much that we began to joke about starting our own ice pop business. It was the 2000s, and food trucks were starting to take off. As regular visitors to our neighborhood farmers markets, we imagined partnering with local farmers to come up with flavor combinations together and introducing folks to something much more thoughtful than the Popsicle we grew up with.

The idea wouldn't go away. We kept talking about it . . . for years. We came up with lists of company names: Tres Hermanos, Frozen Man, and Fria, to name a few that didn't make the cut.

As we studied the *paleta* business model that was prolific in Central America, we noticed how very little went to waste. Super ripe fruit was everywhere, and instead of letting the unsold items spoil, these artisans would transform them into the most delicious *paletas*.

Last but not least, these *paleteros*, the people selling these amazing frozen creations, were out and about in their community, working hard but seemingly having fun. An uncomfortable realization was dawning on me: I wasn't consciously writing a good story with my own work; my story was happening to me.

Back home, I had a good job and was finally getting paid what felt like an adult salary. I had a 401(k) and benefits. When happy hour ended at the bar, I could still afford another round. When I pulled up to the gas station, I could fill my tank all the way up instead of watching the pump numbers turn and trying to get it to stop *right* at $20. I had a decent amount of paid vacation for the first time, and I could finally afford to stay at nicer hotels.

And yet, I honestly didn't understand what my company did. I worked with data and spreadsheets. I spent hours building formulas and testing them. I prepared reports and presentations. My bosses seemed to like me and told me I was doing a good job. Did I know what those reports were for, though? Did I know how the company used them to serve their communities and the world? Did my work really matter in the grand scheme of things?

The truth is, I could have been doing important work, central to the company's mission, and I would have had no idea. No one ever told me, and after a few months, I was too embarrassed to ask.

How do you go into your boss's office after you've worked there three months and ask, "Um, what do we actually do here?"

I wish I had. Now, as a boss, it's the kind of question I hope my team asks me.

But I didn't. So instead, I watched the clock, finished my reports on time, let my brain wander, and waited for five o'clock, when I could get back to doing what I wanted to do.

Then the 2008 recession hit, and layoffs began. People in our building were losing their jobs and emptying their cubicles. I stared at the sports memorabilia around my desk, wondering if I was next.

I didn't feel sad for the company. I felt terrible for my coworkers, but the company felt like a big machine that would just tighten its screws through the crisis and keep pumping out whatever it was we made ad infinitum.

I started to imagine what I might be able to do if I did lose my job. I was already living pretty simply, so it wouldn't require a major overhaul of my expenses to finally try the ice pop business. After all, how hard could it be to make some ice pops? At the very least, wouldn't it make for a great story to tell my grandkids? If I couldn't even explain my corporate job to my friends, what would I say at the end of my life—that I made some great spreadsheets? I wanted more than that.

Then it finally happened. I got the call that I was getting laid off. At that moment, I knew this was my chance to start writing a story I had more control over.

I had a ton of help early on. My friend Dave designed our logo for a couple bucks and the promise of pops for life, my parents and their friends helped set things up and cut fruit, and my brother Nick was there for me every step of the way. He had recently finished law school and was a prosecutor tasked with putting people behind bars, but law could wait. A couple months in, he dropped everything to join full-time. He put in his two-week's notice at the courthouse a few days before our dad's handwritten note urging him to continue his path as a lawyer arrived.

It was exciting, yes, but nothing about those early days was easy. There were a lot of wrong turns and sleepless nights before King of Pops had its first sale. I could tell you about how the brick-and-mortar storefront we had hoped to open didn't work out or how our first ice pop machine, which cost me $6,000 of the $7,000 I'd saved up, never arrived and paid hospital bills for the salesman's sick wife instead. I could tell you how that same salesman finally admitted he'd taken my money in desperation and helped me find a used ice pop machine in Texas a couple weeks before I was supposed to open.

Instead, I'll just tell you this: it was stressful, scary, hard, and a blast, but isn't that true of every great story? You think chasing after your dreams is going to be fun, and it is. But it's the hard kind of fun—the climbing Mount Everest kind of fun, the ultramarathon kind of fun, the kind of fun that chews you up and spits you out the other side as a different person. But I didn't know I was having fun quite yet. I was too close to it; gaining that perspective would take some time.

I had given myself a deadline, for better or for worse, to sell my first pop by April 1, 2010—a full seven months after I'd lost my job. Eventually, when that day came, I pushed my cart, which was wrapped with another company's branding, up to the neighborhood gas station, scribbled my flavors in chalk on a piece of plywood painted black, and said a prayer that customers would show up.

Looking back, it's easy to point out how things sequentially worked out, but living in the story, it doesn't feel so straightforward.

Initially, people were intrigued. I was this random dude in a gas station parking lot trying to sell ice pops out of a tiny pushcart. It wasn't what they were used to seeing, and a few brave ones walked over to check it out as they filled their gas tanks.

I don't remember the words of those first conversations, but I remember feeling terrified as they took their first taste. As I panicked on the inside, I prayed they wouldn't get sick or spit it out in disgust.

I remember selling one woman a Grapefruit Mint pop. I watched her slowly walk back to her car. She sat in the driver's seat, about 30 feet away from me, watching my little pushcart for several minutes as she slowly ate her pop. I tried to pretend like I didn't notice, and when she got back out of her car, I physically turned away from her as she approached. My mind raced. Did she want a refund? Was she from the department of health, here to shut me down? Had it made her sick?

Turns out she loved it and wanted to buy five more to take home for her family to try.

Time flew as I talked with customers, watched them enjoy what we had made, and heard them promise to return. They loved our commitment to simple, fresh, locally sourced ingredients. They loved the unique flavor combinations like Tangerine Basil,

Pineapple Habanero, Blackberry Ginger Lemonade, and Banana Puddin'. And they loved that we wanted to bring some good vibes and make a difference in our community. Those first few weeks, I couldn't stop smiling.

I also couldn't keep up. We were having a moment. The stars had aligned in such a way that people were driving from across the state to wait in line to buy pops from our tiny cart in the corner of a gas station parking lot. Some days ended earlier than planned, as I would sell out of pops, and if I hadn't, when I closed the umbrella and started to pack things up, a group would scurry up, hoping they hadn't missed out. I was experiencing a completely different level of exhaustion. I had always been active. In high school, I played soccer and basketball and ran cross-country. My dad did his best to show me what a hard day's work felt like, but what my brother Nick and I went through that first year was on a whole new level. Even so, my head was spinning with ideas.

We would find ourselves tinkering with every aspect of the pops we were making at all hours. We went to farmers markets to get fruits at the perfect level of ripeness, then we would take them back to our kitchen, cut off the rind of melons and pineapple, peel and dice mangos, remove the pits of peaches (there's nothing worse than leaving even a sliver of peach pit in, which ruins the whole batch), rinse and blend berries, bruise mint and basil to bring out the flavor, then chop them up before dropping them into a steaming kettle to make a new simple syrup, slice and juice limes and lemons and other citrus fruits. Every fruit had a different process, and our arms would get sore from repeating the same motions over and over. It was hard work, but after all the prep came the fun part: coming up with ideas for flavors and mixing ingredients to create a new pop, scaling flavors to get the exact right mix, then of course tasting everything and talking about what we liked or didn't, then starting over with a new idea.

It was overwhelming to think about all the flavor combinations we could create. I understood so clearly what we were offering our customers—and they were falling in love with what we were making.

Who knew a tiny ice pop cart in the corner of a gas station parking lot had the potential to tell an epic story and make a difference?

And just like that, King of Pops was born. There was no going back.

WHY YOU'RE NOT HAVING FUN

Can you honestly say you can't wait to get back to work tomorrow? When was the last time work was fun?

When you begin a new job, you're engaged and curious as you meet the challenge of figuring out your role and responsibilities. You pay attention to coworkers and actively network to see where you fit. You worry excessively about the first few projects you complete. But what happens when that initial burst of energy ends?

What happens when you've created your 62nd spreadsheet, and the person in the cubicle next to you is annoying, and you feel like you're on a treadmill to nowhere with your best days passing you by? What happens then?

Nothing.

And that's the problem. You keep slogging through it, either because you have bills to pay and mouths to feed, or maybe you just don't know how to do something different.

If you've ever felt disengaged at work, you're not alone. According to Gallup, only a third of US workers felt engaged at their jobs in 2022. That's sobering. It means two-thirds of us are disengaged. We don't feel curious or connected. When there are challenges, they feel pointless or arbitrary. No fun.

You're going to spend about a third of your life at work. Wouldn't you rather enjoy it?

Over the last 20 years, some companies have gone to extreme lengths to help their employees do just that. Surprisingly, despite all the perks, employee turnover at these companies hasn't slowed at all. It's almost as if people don't want to have fun at work, or maybe, just maybe, perks alone don't boost engagement and enjoyment as much as we wish they would.

So why are you disengaged and distracted, wasting time? Why aren't you having fun at work?

The short answer is because you don't want to or don't know how. Your work lacks meaning, and that makes it hard to get excited and curious each day. It makes it impossible to meet challenges or grow. You're not having fun because you don't know the story of your work.

As I started King of Pops, I realized that every pop I made, every conversation I had with a customer, every credit card I swiped, every team meeting, and every spreadsheet I filled out was telling a story. And what was amazing was that the story could be a good story, full of meaning and purpose. It could, in other words, be fun! Or that story could be boring.

Sometimes we approach work as a to-do list instead of as an adventure to take. The to-do list approach burns us out and steals our enjoyment. No one is going to look at their list of to-dos (even if they are completed) and say, "Wow, that was a trip!"

I love to-do lists, but I don't want my life to be a series of disconnected tasks, and neither do you. I want to engage daily in a way that reminds me that these are the good ol' days—days I will remember and look back on with gratitude and joy. That's why knowing the story you're living is important.

A company's story is not just the end product or service it offers. It's the whole narrative it tells the world about why it exists, who it serves, how it does things, and the values it represents. The story is about how an organization finds meaning in the work it shares with the world.

Here's the surprising truth: the foundation of fun starts with an epic story. *Your* epic story.

You aren't having fun at work because you aren't invested in a meaningful story—you don't see how your personal story intersects with your work's story. Yet.

For work to be fun, you need to feel engaged, curious, and challenged. You need to feel like you have a place in your work community, that your contribution matters. That's why your epic story is so important. Story is where engagement begins.

Insisting on turning your life, including your work life, into a story you're proud to share is the mindset you need to have in order to make your work fun.

My story as a company founder may be different from yours, but the recipe is the same.

Just like making an amazing pop, it starts with the right ingredients. First, you must pick a goal that you are inspired by. Think hard about what a good life looks like to you. And eventually write it down.

From there, the pursuit of that goal naturally brings up all kinds of complications and roadblocks.

These are the steps you'll want to skip—like breaking down a box of watermelons or squeezing hundreds of lemons—you'll want to just be done with them, but they are crucial.

Once you've sourced and prepped delicious ingredients, it's easy to mix them together and make something delicious.

But what if, after all that, the pop or your story isn't as amazing as you hoped?

There is a good chance you'll come very close to failing, or you might straight up fail. That is OK because chances are you'll realize a new audacious goal and repeat the process, or you might end up like me, making ice pops for the rest of your life.

WHAT'S A STORY?

Story is how we make sense of life. In movies, books, and TV shows, we love characters who want something so much they are willing to make bold choices and act in the face of conflict to reach for their goal. The pursuit of that goal changes the character, forcing them to see themselves and reality anew.

Similarly, when a person pursues a goal in an audacious way, we're riveted, whether it's SpaceX pursuing its goal to send humans to Mars or the coffee shop down the street raising money for the neighboring school. We want to tell a great story with our lives. That was the realization that pushed me to take a risk on King of Pops. When I imagined myself sitting on the front porch as an old man, I realized I cared little about the view, the fanciness of the porch, or the type of car parked in the driveway. I just wanted to be able to tell better stories about my life. I wanted to do something that I felt mattered.

Stories aren't just a series of random events that happen to you. The best stories include choices, change, and meaning. They start with a goal: something you want so much you're willing to take risks to reach it. As you pursue that goal, things get in the way that force you to make choices. Things happen that make the experience better than you could have ever imagined, and others come out of nowhere and shake you to the core. Those experiences change you and help you understand yourself and the world.

Let's look again at the story I was writing before King of Pops:

An entry-level analyst joins a company, making spreadsheets and reports. At first, the challenge of learning the job, and his need to pay rent, keeps him engaged. But the work quickly becomes redundant. Sure, he sits in meetings where people give inspiring talks and set productivity and profit goals. But at the end of each one, he heads back to his desk, creates another spreadsheet that he hopes is closer to what the boss wants, and checks the weather for his weekend hike, grateful he has enough money to meet friends for drinks later. He leaves work behind each day without another thought.

Do you see what's missing? I had no goal, aside from making money, and no real choices that matter. The work part of my life was devoid of meaning. I was having fun everywhere except at work.

Imagine if I'd been led to understand what we did as a company, challenged to set a personal goal that required risk, real choices, and creativity. Imagine if the company told me why the work they were doing was important to the world beyond its shareholders.

Your story at work is about more than just knowing the company's origin story. It's about aligning with the current values, setting a worthy goal, and pursuing that goal—leading to a story worth telling. And if you don't feel like your company fits that mold, it's about working to make positive change there or leaving to find somewhere you can do that.

But remember, leaving is the easy part. The real work, the real fun work, is in creating positive change from wherever your current seat is.

This can happen anywhere. I could have done it at the giant insurance company, at my newspaper job in Idaho, or at the dining hall I worked at in college.

For me, it took leaving those jobs behind to find what mattered to me, but I wish I had done my part to make those jobs more fun while I was there.

DOES KNOWING THE STORY REALLY MATTER?

I used to think the story behind your work didn't really matter. I certainly wouldn't have connected it with fun. Don't get me wrong: growing up, I had pretty fun jobs. I was a referee for kids' soccer games, sold random stuff on eBay, and in college I hawked trays of cotton candy and snow cones in the stands at Atlanta Braves games.

These were cool jobs. But the story behind them, the meaning? That wasn't on my mind much.

That changed a couple years after starting King of Pops. I learned about a smallish company called Zingerman's in Ann Arbor, Michigan, which had turned a beloved deli into an internationally loved group of businesses that oozed with story and meaning. Although they have fans worldwide, each of their businesses is located in Ann Arbor. This unique choice was written into their vision early on.

After reading about them in Bo Burlingham's *Small Giants*, I booked a trip with my brother to see it firsthand and attend a ZingTrain training.

At the time, King of Pops was starting to gain some momentum, selling hundreds of thousands of pops every year. Our team had grown from just me and my brother Nick to a group of 10 or so people.

And yet, after every summer, when the weather got cold and people stopped buying pops, we worried, "Is this it? Is everyone going to forget us? When we open our stand in the spring, is anyone even going to come?"

We had not thought about what things should look like 10 years into the future. We were busily trying to survive, making the same mistake the businesses we'd worked at before had made. We didn't have a vision, a story of what we hoped the future would look like.

When it was just me and my brother, it was easy to communicate and get excited about what was next, which was usually done late at night while we were frantically making as many pops as we could to sell the next day! But as we grew, sharing our plans for the company, why we existed, and just keeping people engaged in general became more and more challenging.

So we went to Ann Arbor, to Zingerman's, where they had been doing this successfully for over 30 years and were still growing. What we saw at Zingerman's blew me away. At every level of the company, from the executives to the managers down to the dishwasher or the woman excitedly telling customers about the bread options for sandwiches, the energy was electric.

I selfishly wanted the same.

The lessons taught in ZingTrain are top-notch, and there are nonstop aha moments during the course of the training. Putting a framework around creating a vision was extremely helpful. I remember catching myself time and time again that first session, dreaming a few degrees beyond the realm of possibility. It sounds strange looking back on it, but the best way I can explain how I felt in those rooms was a shortness of breath.

I felt so inspired in those moments that I worried I would not properly capture the work that I knew needed to be done. I'd write down things that would sound ridiculous to repeat once I'd left the fairy dust–sprinkled confines of our classroom. I couldn't help it.

But there was something that I saw outside of the official training that put things properly in perspective. During their stay, it's common for people to visit Zingerman's Roadhouse, a James Beard Award–winning restaurant that is part of the Zingerman's Community of Businesses.

We were excited to try the food, and when we showed up, we were shown to our table. Before too long, I saw someone who looked familiar pouring water for customers, and I did a double take. When I realized it was one of our instructors that day—in fact, Ari Weinzweig himself, CEO of the entire company—I was shocked. There he was, head of an $80 million-plus food empire, pouring water, sometimes silently, sometimes chatting with customers, sometimes asking attendees of the workshop what their biggest takeaways were. For me, I didn't need him to ask me. It was this. Here was a guy who could be anywhere in the world, selecting to spend his evening in the business. He was simultaneously showing the vision of his organization and that work could be fun in the simplest of acts, and I knew I had so much more to learn. I saw firsthand that I didn't need to think of my own version of superfluous work benefits for my employees, but instead focus on creating an inspiring vision, then get busy working toward it.

Ari was demonstrating his version of servant leadership, but what rang true most for me was that he was at the level that I was aspiring to get to one day, yet he wasn't in the background pulling strings, disconnected from the day-to-day work. He couldn't have been more "in it."

That moment rejected the viral-but-untrue mantras that winning means scaling your business as fast as possible. Without saying anything, he showed me that the work being fun was more important than the perks that come with it.

It wasn't long before I was back in Ann Arbor. Our company had tripled in size, our headcount was just over 30, and six people from the King of Pops team accompanied me. Just as I had learned so much about the importance of a company's vision and story, I could see it on the faces of my team as they caught the same ideas, then the surprise when they watched Ari pouring water and making that vision real for them. I don't know if Ari pours water every night (I hope not), but he has fun being there.

When we got back to our hotel after wrapping up our second day, the absurd-but-amazing ideas were flowing—only this time, it was not just in my head. We couldn't stop talking about what we were learning and what we wanted to share with the rest of the company back home in Atlanta.

Prior to this, we had the energy and buy-in from our team, but it was mostly chaotic and unfocused—we knew we could do more in our community, but we weren't sure how to balance that with our sense that "real" business still needed to take place in order to succeed.

So we snuck into an empty conference room at the hotel we were staying in, borrowed their whiteboard, and started brainstorming our vision late into the night. Enjoyment and fun kept coming up as core values—we wanted to be a place where people loved to work and where customers loved our product and experience. We didn't want our brand to be about a product alone, but a positive, silly, and weird part of the community that people who didn't even like desserts loved.

We got back to Atlanta and began to work through our ideas with a larger committee of team members, refining the vision and story. We set a date for a company-wide meeting to read the vision together.

But when I got in front of the rest of the team, who had not just been through a two-day vision indoctrination, I was sweating with nervousness. What had seemed like a great idea in snow-covered Michigan now seemed kind of silly and naive standing in a circle in front of 30 or so people in sunny Atlanta.

Would the rest of the team be on board? Or had we gotten carried away by enthusiasm?

Once we gathered, I read the letter from me to the company that introduced our vision. I hoped more than anything that they "got it"—that they understood what we were doing, that we were beginning to tell the story of what King of Pops could be if we put in the work.

You can read the entire letter and vision statement we crafted in the appendix of this book, but let me pull a few bits from the letter and a section from the vision, so you get a sense of the story we wanted to tell with our company. I read my letter out loud, then members of our team read the different sections of our Rainbow Umbrella Vision for 2030.

Excerpts from the letter written by Steve Carse to King of Pops, and the team-created vision:

To those who refuse to just exist,

In 2010 we didn't start with a formal business plan. There wasn't a focus group that selected the rainbow umbrella that now casts shade over hundreds of pushcarts throughout the South. Our professional culinary experience was nonexistent.

So how did we get here? The reality is that I was 25, and the idea of selling pops for the summer seemed like fun. We chose the first rainbow umbrella because it was in stock, and we could afford it. As for making pops, well, we just hoped we could figure that out.

. . . However, what Nick and I started was only the beginning of what we have now. The "secret," our single greatest achievement, has been inspiring a group of employees who connect with what is going on. What started as a job for so many is now so much more. Our constant sacrifice is draining and exhilarating at the same time . . .

Let's never stop pushing each other. These are the good ol' days.

Here is a glance at what we all have to look forward to in 2030.

Rainbow Umbrella 2030 Vision

This vision verbalizes our core values and begins to establish why we operate.

✦ Be Thoughtful ✦ Get Sweaty ✦ Good Vibes Only ✦
✦ Wear the Shirt ✦ Stay Hungry ✦ Get It Done ✦

Our Neighbors Smile When They See Us

Every year we've started and ended the season with some type of thank-you to our community. Typically it includes free pops and a handful of other ideas that seem fun, silly, or strange in the moment. The simple gesture goes a long way in explaining how and why we operate.

If we can consistently sweeten the lives of our neighbors and enjoy doing it, we all win.

This year is special. Our 20th year has come to a close, and the similarities to the early days outnumber the differences. We still host a party, the informal nature is still endearing, and we are still giving away pops to anyone who will have one.

What started as a King of Pops celebration now incorporates bits and pieces from each brand under the Rainbow Umbrella. Attendance is optional, but employees new and old rarely miss the occasion. A group that has never met has an *immediate bond, laughing and comparing stories about what has changed and what is still the same. Most importantly, they talk excitedly about what is to come.*

The same enthusiasm permeates our organization every day. Significant others and friends have gotten used to hearing work talk hours after we've officially "clocked out" for the day. It's not always our fault—if you're within a couple blocks of HQ and you happen to be wearing a company T-shirt, it's pretty common for a stranger to walk up and start a conversation about the latest project.

It's nice to be loved, and our response is to love back. We like to have fun, and for us it's more fun when we invite our neighbors. We're active in the community far beyond our business, whether it's a huge event like Field Day (which is essentially just a staff party that we decided to invite the city to), the annual field trips that dozens of inner-city schools take to a King of Crops outpost, the latest community service project that was conceived by our Do-Gooder committee, or any of the hundreds of new, half-baked ideas we try each year that make just enough sense to work.

As I watched the faces of our employees as they listened to the vision, I thought my heart would beat out of my chest.

I had worried that people would snicker, roll their eyes, and blow it off. Or worse, just zone out.

But the opposite happened.

I saw people smile knowingly. I saw team members nodding along with the parts that struck home. Some people barked with laughter. All around the circle, there was a very positive energy. I think part of it was they could tell we really cared and had poured our hearts into this, but it also sounded pretty cool, like a place they'd want to spend their time building.

The truth is, for most of the company, this was probably not that memorable a moment. A boss was reading a document about why the company was cool. But it struck a chord with some right away, and as we continued to refer back to it year after year, the things that they said would happen up in Ann Arbor started to take root.

Suddenly we weren't just placing thousands of Popsicle sticks into an aligner, managing shipments, cleaning carts and repairing umbrellas—we were fulfilling the vision. It helped us understand why the work we were doing would matter today, tomorrow, and in 15 years.

We're now a decade into our 15-year vision. With only five years until we are hoping to realize our vision, a lot of the content still rings true, but other pieces are now most likely not going to happen in the time frame.

I feel a bit uneasy as I read these sections aloud in meetings nowadays, but I push through and make lighthearted jokes about it once I'm done. For example, there is a part of the vision that states, "Steve still offers up his condo for visiting employees." I used to Airbnb this condo, and it was easy to make it available. Now it has a full-time tenant, and I don't think he'd be too excited about this arrangement.

Even the bits and pieces that aren't going to happen paint a picture of what our company is all about. If it is your first day and you read this vision, you get a sense of where our heart is at and why this thing matters. Specific details make a great vision stand out, but it is the combination of all those details that make it something worth working toward.

The work is never done. We will never achieve our vision, and before the date we've imagined arrives, we will begin the process of writing a new vision with updated moonshot goals and ideas that demonstrate where we want to go.

The fun isn't in the destination; it's in the journey to get there.

THE STORY MATTERS

As humans, we crave the meaning that stories provide. Real meaning—meaning that can't be distilled to a mission statement posted on the wall of a breakroom coffee station or annual report binder.

It's meaning that gets us up in the morning. It's meaning that keeps us engaged and curious. It's meaning that sustains us when we feel like giving up when things get hard.

Humans can endure all manner of hardship, sacrifice, and even suffering if we know why it matters.

Maybe you wouldn't consider your time at work a sacrifice, but it is an investment. Your time is the most precious resource you have—one that can't be renewed or repurchased.

You might not describe your experience at work as suffering, but if you are unfulfilled, disinterested, and checked out, then over time, you are likely to become resentful and bitter, unproductive and miserable.

When you make a significant sacrifice for work, perhaps even suffer, the one thing that can help you push through those difficult seasons is the story you're telling yourself about why it matters. Meaning helps you stay engaged when you'd rather check out. And if you're tempted to ask if that really makes a difference for business, consider this: companies with engaged workforces outperform competitors in earnings per share by 147% (Gallup).

Engagement.

It's everything, and too many managers and companies think it means "making employees happy," which is why we see the increasingly outrageous benefits. Free snacks, massage chairs, and foosball tables might seem fun for a minute, but they don't help when you're up against a tight deadline, working with a challenging client, or implementing something new that might not work in a bold attempt to solve a serious problem.

It's story that provides authentic engagement because it actively requires you to do something real to achieve a worthy goal that matters. Story requires your unique talents, viewpoint, and enthusiasm. Story requires risk and bold decisions that have consequences.

This is what truly engages people and creates fun: knowing their choices make a difference. When you know your decisions have real consequences, you get curious about the problem, you get creative when you bump up against complications, and you lean into your strengths to solve it in a way that is uniquely your own. Even when things don't work out the way you planned, you have a hell of a story to tell as you iterate and try again.

That opening day for King of Pops at the gas station in Atlanta, I hadn't been counting down the time, bored and disengaged. True, I did have to stop to use the bathroom, but that was because I couldn't hold it any longer.

I asked a customer standing around if she could keep an eye on the cart for me, and I rushed in and out—not wanting to miss a moment. This alone was a completely different experience from my previous work, in which the restroom break had been more about taking a break, a reprieve, a moment for yourself than the actual biological stuff.

I half-jogged in and out, not wanting to miss a moment or a sale. I would have run but didn't want to look ridiculous.

Why?

At the time, I might have said: it was fun.

But what made it fun? There are several things, but the most important one is that I knew the story. I knew what we were selling our customers. I knew how those products were made. I knew why we'd sourced the ingredients we had. I had used my own hands to prep those ingredients. And I knew why we minimized waste, to do the work in a way that left Atlanta better. It meant something to me, and I was able to communicate that meaning to our customers as well.

We were after Unexpected Moments of Happiness (our company purpose), and while I might have approached that goal with my experiences in Central America in mind, every one of our employees and Cartrepreneur franchisees has pursued that goal in their own way, helping write them into the King of Pops story forever.

Whatever job you're in right now, do you know the story? Do you know what you offer and why? Do you know why your work matters to you and your community?

Don't brush it off and pretend what your organization does isn't important. A worthwhile purpose does not have to be unique. In fact, most of them are some version of "make the world a better place." But if we can make ice pops matter, you can certainly understand the value you offer in your position. From slinging ice pops to making sandwiches, selling cars to filing medical billing— all work is more fun when you know what it means.

YOUR PERSONAL WORK JOURNEY

Getting involved in and buying into your organization's story is key for having fun, but this is just one part of your personal work story.

At every moment, in parallel, you're participating in your organization's story and writing your own personal story. A little later in this book, I'll make the case for being patient and spending time at your various places of employment, but the truth is you'll have a handful of jobs in your life.

I hope King of Pops is the remainder of my life's pursuit, but even so, it is not my whole work story. An important part of my personal work story was starting in the journalism industry, leaving it too early to work at a large corporation, getting laid off, and then starting my own thing.

For most people, there is a sweet spot. I haven't met anyone who proudly changes jobs every six months. At the same time, if the story you've envisioned for yourself is in no way related to where you currently work, you should probably start planning your exit.

Most people don't put the energy into thinking about their personal work journey holistically. They obsess over where they want to be next but usually stop there.

When I took a moment to finally reflect on the big picture after losing my job, before starting King of Pops, the story I wanted to write at that point in my life involved more risk and adventure. I wanted my work to be entrepreneurial and fun.

I didn't have a crystal-clear picture of what my work story would look like. These were just themes, but they informed my decisions.

If you take the time to come up with your vision, and ideally write it down, it will provide guardrails to help make decisions going forward a little easier. For example, I got called by recruiters in the insurance industry after I got laid off. I even flew to Boston to interview at another large insurance company, but by that point I'd decided I wanted more risk and adventure in my life. After all, the insurance industry is all about mitigating risk.

In a practical sense, your resume is the basis of your work story. If you already know the story you want to write, pull it out and review your last few stops. Are they serving your bigger purpose? Can you stitch together the part of a great story with the bulleted summaries that represent how you've spent large chunks of your life?

Is there something else you'd want to see there? If you know the next few stops you'd like to make, go ahead and write them down in a different color, then use that as a reference for your personal work vision.

Maybe these are things you can do within your current organization, or maybe you'll have to look elsewhere.

Once you start telling a better story about yourself and your work and having more fun, it's almost impossible to go back. As Donald Miller wrote in his book *A Million Miles in a Thousand Years*, "Once you live a good story, you get a taste for a kind of meaning in life, and you can't go back to being normal; you can't go back to meaningless scenes stitched together by the forgettable thread of wasted time."

How to Live a Great Story

The hardest part of consciously writing a positive story about your life is starting. As humans, we've evolved to avoid risk and dangerous situations. We're very good at imagining with great clarity all the bad things that can happen, but we aren't so good at imagining best-case scenarios.

I couldn't have imagined all the amazing things that happened in my life after starting King of Pops, but I know the practice of landing on themes and writing down specifics of what I hoped might happen propelled me to live a better story.

All we can do is show up and put forth our best effort. Life is beautiful in that way.

As kids, we imagine ourselves doing all sorts of things. We play doctor, obsess over construction equipment, and dream of being an astronaut. And yet, for some reason, we stop imagining what work could be once we're in it. We allow ourselves to feel stuck even though we aren't.

Chasing a dream allows you to feel connected, and when you're plugged in with a clear goal and purpose, you'll realize you're also having a lot of fun.

Some of you might already be CEOs or entrepreneurs with a lot of control. Others might be new hires who aren't even sure what your company does yet. Wherever you are, though, you can begin telling a better story at work and start enjoying your work more.

Early in our careers, we often have less of a say in writing the story of the organization we are working at. That changes as we gain experience, but it is never fully one or the other.

Nearly everyone answers to someone else sometimes. As a business owner, I don't want to send in quarterly updates to the bank, but that isn't up to me. It's something I have to do.

While you alone hold the pen for your personal work story, the organization is writing its own story with the help of everyone in it. The next two sections are about how to show up and contribute wherever you are currently.

When It's Not Up to You

Ideally, the leaders in your organization have coordinated an exceptional onboarding experience that helps you understand the company, its story, its current course, and the goals you can set and meet to join and expand the story.

But even if they don't, you can still thrive, tell a great story, and have fun. Start by asking, "What do we actually do here?" and keep patiently asking until you fully understand what your work is and why it matters. Keep an eye out for coworkers who are enjoying their job, and pay attention.

Refuse to fake it like I did. If you want to feel engaged, if you want to have fun at work, you can't fake it. Stay curious and keep asking questions while you get your footing.

Find out how the company was started. See if there's any company lore that's been lost. Ask people about their most meaningful interactions with coworkers or customers.

Research the community where you work. What's the history of the area? When was it established, and how has it changed? What interesting monuments, markers, or buildings are in the area? What annual events draw visitors? What are locals' favorite haunts and hotspots, and why?

When you want a great story and it isn't up to you, consider starting here:

- If there is a part of the business you find interesting, ask if you can get involved in it, even if it's just for an hour a week.

- Are there parts of the business you don't understand? Be curious. Ask your manager for more information, and if they don't know, ask their boss.

- Find a lane, and be useful. If you become an expert in an area (even if it is a very small area), you'll soon be irreplaceable, and opportunities will continue to arise.

- Be patient. Realize that there is a lot happening behind the scenes, but find a way to thoughtfully ask questions, even if you don't get answers right away. Ask again and again, always in a thoughtful way, until things make sense. Asking questions requires no additional training, but it will show you care.

- Ask yourself, "What is the story I'm hoping to tell from my time in my current role?"

A quick bit of bonus advice if you're interviewing for a new role: it can be compelling to paint the picture of how your personal work vision complements the story of the organization you are hoping to join. Just be careful that you don't frame your desire for the position too heavily around what you're looking to gain. A for-profit business is ultimately going to be more interested in how you are going to contribute to their success.

It's nice for hiring managers to know that a position you are interested in is your dream job, but that alone doesn't make you more qualified than other candidates. In the context of being a productive employee at work, it's about your contribution to the organization's purpose.

When It's Up to You

As a leader, you have a lot of power to help your people tell a great story because you communicate the vision for your business. You help determine the meaning that will drive engagement and fun for every single person. Write it down, so you are connected to it and feel accountable to it.

What is your company or business doing in practical terms? What value does it offer? How does it make the world a better place? Why did you start the company, or why do you believe in it enough to lead it now?

Paint the picture of what success looks like. Throw in a few details for fun. And if you want to get really inspired, go to a visioning seminar (I recommend ZingTrain).

If you don't know the answer to these questions, your team won't know them either. These questions help you establish the stakes—what happens when you win and what happens when you lose—in more than monetary terms.

It's also your responsibility to provide opportunities for others to speak into your vision or goal at an appropriate level. At King of Pops, we host an annual symposium where every member of the company has an opportunity to share ideas, and it's my job to listen, truly listen, to what the group says and ideally set up a way to try their ideas. That symposium isn't the only place we let ideas circulate, but it is an intentional, visible reminder that each employee's ideas are valuable and heard.

Every employee is initially introduced to our 2030 vision, written as a story in the future, during orientation and then again at the annual symposium. It's something we do over and over, telling and retelling the story. It's worthwhile to make sure the communication is clear.

If you have established mission and purpose statements, how are you making them practical and real instead of stale signage posted around your building? Set a reminder on your calendar to live out your purpose. Consider building your mission and purpose statements into your performance review as a conversation point and an opportunity to reemphasize how important they are.

Do you have an onboarding process that helps new hires understand your vision and purpose? *Harvard Business Review* found that companies with robust onboarding processes that help new hires understand how they fit within a company's existing culture and purpose have far higher rates of retention and job satisfaction. Onboarding has to be more than watching videos and clicking through a slide show. How are you inviting new hires into a story? What audacious goals will they set, and how will you empower their decision-making?

As a leader, you set the example and the course for everyone else. Don't get caught up on having the "deepest," most unique or thoughtful purpose or mission, but be sure to have one. Most meaningful company purposes come back to helping others.

Here are some additional questions to help you start to work on writing that epic story:

- What is your vision for your business, and why does it matter?
- What stories already guide your company? Does everyone know them? Do any need to be changed?
- How are you inviting your team into decision-making?
- How are you creating opportunities for people to tell better stories with their work?
- What is the story you're hoping to tell from your time leading?

CHAPTER 2

These Are the Good Ol' Days

THESE ARE THE GOOD OL' DAYS

King of Pops pushcarts are the standard design seen throughout Latin America—an insulated, stainless-steel box with some wheels, a handlebar, and a few openings on the top.

Their beauty is in their simplicity.

They don't plug in but instead rely on cold plates or dry ice to keep things frozen.

This means there is less to break. And it also means that each time you go to an event, you're effectively starting a timer that, once expired, will result in a worthless puddle of former ice pops at the bottom of your cart.

Over the years, we've gotten quite good at avoiding the puddles and preserving the pops. So much so that when we go to out-of-town music festivals like Bonnaroo, we pack thousands of pops in pallet-sized coolers with enough dry ice to keep them frozen for a week. For weekend events like this, we arrive on a Wednesday and won't sell our last pop until Sunday.

We use dry ice because refrigerated trucks are prone to breaking on the hottest days of the year. Unsurprisingly, calling the freezer repairman to a campground in the middle of the night with tens of thousands of festivalgoers eagerly waiting for the headliner to come on has a low success rate.

Science doesn't break, so we've decided that at these high-stakes, low-infrastructure events, we want to control our own destiny by using dry ice to keep things appropriately frozen.

There is a learning curve when it comes to the ins and outs of dry ice. And, unfortunately, some good pops were lost as I got up to speed.

One of my most memorable dry ice lessons happened during King of Pops' first summer.

Quite a few of our best customers early on were tattoo artists. I'm tattooless myself, but for whatever reason, the classic car, Betty Boop–type of tattoo enthusiasts were drawn to King of Pops. I was working at the cart that first year when one of my highly tattooed regulars invited me to bring the cart to an event called Drive-Invasion.

It was a late-summer overnight BYOB event at the Starlight Drive-In Theatre, featuring a car show, 20 or so bands, and four movies that started once the last band ended and played until the sun came up the next morning.

It sounded interesting: an all-night festival in a drive-in parking lot certainly aligned with my overall goal of living a story I wanted to tell. Without thinking twice, I let them know I would be there.

When the day of the event arrived, I coaxed my friend Tyler into joining me by promising a case of beer and lots of great people watching. We showed up at 11 AM with a couple of lawn chairs, the beer, and a cart full of six hundred pops on dry ice.

We'd both been to the Starlight before, but never when the sun was shining. It looked dystopian as sound techs set up stages and organizers scurried around, getting the last details set.

There are several factors that impact how long your dry ice will keep your pops frozen—ambient temperature, the time the cart tops are open, and how tightly you've packed your pops against each other are the ones that usually matter the most.

That morning, I had confidently packed the cart with these factors in mind.

However, this gigantic parking lot in mid-August was not aligned with my goal of keeping pops frozen. The acres of uninterrupted blacktop turned out to be an X factor I had not considered. Within a couple hours, as the August sun rose to the middle of the sky, it became clear that my rainbow umbrella was no defense for the heat reflecting up from the asphalt.

As a result, my dry ice was depleting at record speed. What's more, I didn't bring water, and the muggy heat and social anxiety were leading me to drink beer at an ill-advised pace.

I watched nervously as attendees settled into their tent compounds. Plenty of people were walking by, promising to come back later in the day, but by 4 PM, I had only made a few sales, and my pops were starting to "sweat." Tiny beads of water were forming on the outsides of the wrappers. Even an ice pop novice knows this is not a good sign.

There was nobody to call to save the day, so I went into deal-making mode. Normally, we leave the cart in one high-traffic spot and wait for people to come to us. This makes sense at most events most of the time. Eventually, the majority of the people will walk the grounds and stumble upon you.

I skew toward introversion and get uncomfortable walking up to strangers to strike up an unprovoked conversation. However, our normal stationary strategy clearly wasn't going to work on this day. I couldn't bear to watch six hundred pops, a day's worth of production at that time, melt.

I also couldn't afford it.

So Tyler and I embarked on an odyssey that I will never forget, pushing the cart up and down the rows of makeshift compounds, past classic cars, and through crowds of some of the most interesting people I've ever met.

In that moment, selling those pops seemed like the only thing that mattered. As I'm prone to do, I asked the man upstairs, or whoever might be listening, for some help: "Just let me sell these pops, and I won't ask for anything else."

The adrenaline pushed me out of my comfort zone.

I gave a man with a parrot on his shoulder free pops to walk along with us, with his bird saying "I love you" and "What's your name?" to potential customers.

I started guaranteeing that they'd love the pops, and if they didn't, I'd give them their money back.

As the pops got softer, my desperation grew.

I made deals like "buy 10, get five free." And sometimes I just begged.

By 6 PM, with my inventory running low, I found myself with a line of customers.

I sold my last pop by 7:30 PM, and my prayer (for that day, at least) was answered. I was in no shape to drive, so Tyler and I enjoyed the festival and got a little bit of sleep in our lawn chairs.

It was, once again, one of my favorite days ever. (And it was work!)

Urgency is exhilarating and exhausting.

We need these shots of adrenaline to do meaningful work and get through big projects, but once complete, we return to more of the same. In the moment, I assumed that once I had overcome the drive-in debacle, things would settle into easy or "be normal."

However, that is almost never the case.

It's as if you're on the track team, doing the hurdles, and you're only aware of the first hurdle in the set of 10.

A solid strategy is to focus on them one at a time, but in the back of your mind, you're aware that another nine are there once you get over the first. Once you get through the first problem, there will be another one and another one and another one.

It's amazing how many times we can learn this lesson.

If I can get through this one project, everything will be OK. If I get this promotion, I'll be set. If I get this new car, I'll be happy. If my kid gets into this school, nothing else will matter.

I do not know how to make this feeling go away. However, acknowledging its existence does offer some peace.

Looking back, pushing the cart with melting pops through the drive-in was a highlight of my year. I met so many cool people and created an unforgettable story with my friend. I have a fond memory of the time, even if I didn't enjoy it in the moment. I was too busy being terrified and praying for a miracle.

Hard work feels like this quite often. And if we're busy thinking that something else will be better, we inhibit ourselves from having fun in the moment.

We have this cheesy saying at King of Pops that I thought I came up with for a speech during one of our end-of-year field days. Turns out, it's all over the internet, stitched on pillows, printed on T-shirts and mugs.

It's just six words, and the hope is that they remind us of this lesson when we need it most.

These are the good ol' days.

You can interpret it a few ways, but to me it's a reminder to live in the present. Don't romanticize the past or wait longingly for the future.

This is it. Right now is everything, so enjoy it.

It is very unlikely that the future you're looking forward to will be more enjoyable than your current state. Different? Yes. Better? Probably not. There will be problems. There will be things you don't have that you want. Things you don't want to do that you have to do. And there will be joy.

Give or take a few brief peaks and dips, this is what life is made of. Once you feel like you're writing a great story, it's natural to want to skip to the end, to get to the conclusion faster. If you're reading a good book, you might stay up all night to do just that, but in life we're all reading at the same speed. We can't speed up time. And truthfully, it's passing us by pretty darn fast as it is.

The feelings you feel right now, whether they are pain, anxiety, excitement, fun, or most likely some combination of all of those, are bits and pieces of what make a compelling story.

People regularly reminisce about the past fondly, but what you're living right now will be your past soon enough. When you realize that *these are the good ol' days*, you are reminiscing in real time. You are giving the moment right now the attention it deserves, and you are going to have more fun as a result. If you're enjoying the moment instead of looking forward to the future, you'll inherently be more patient.

Just remember, suspense is a good thing. It's a requirement for a great story. If it has been a while since you've felt uneasy about what is going on around you, then it's time to get to work on your story.

WORK *FOMO*

Once you realize you're truly living out the good ol' days of your story right now, you'll start to look at new opportunities differently. Hopefully you'll realize that the place in your career you are occupying right now is not where you'll end up but is pretty amazing in its own ways.

In the moment, it seems like the place you want to end up is going to be so much more fun, but the truth is, it's not. It's just different. What you're really dealing with is FOMO.

FOMO, fear of missing out, is most often a fairly innocent, day-to-day malady.

It's something businesses use to sell more of their limited-time widgets, and friends use it to talk you into going to parties you shouldn't go to when you have to wake up early the next morning.

When I graduated college, I had a more serious strain of FOMO: "work FOMO." My job was OK, but I was constantly questioning if I was advancing quickly enough. I regularly wondered, "Would a different job be better?"

I couldn't help but think about the other places I could be working, and I felt like I needed to figure it all out right away.

As a result of work FOMO, I didn't handle my first full-time job out of college that well. I quit before I absorbed the lessons and without truly giving it a chance, and to this day, I regret leaving so quickly.

After graduating from the University of Georgia (go Dawgs), I applied to every sportswriting job available in the country. After some interviews, I got two offers. One was in LaGrange, Georgia, a dusty suburb of a suburb a couple of hours from where I grew up. The other was in Idaho Falls, Idaho, a primarily Mormon town that happened to be on the doorstep to some of the most beautiful nature in the country. I'm prewired for adventure, and I figured going west would be a better story. So I packed my things into my brown Pontiac Grand Prix and drove to Idaho.

I grew up playing sports and love most of them. A huge Bill Simmons fan, I dreamed of sharing my witty, well-crafted opinions on professional sports with the masses.

That dream would have to wait. Other than rodeo, there aren't any professional sports to speak of in Idaho Falls. I spent most of my time driving around the state covering high school sports.

Still, it was invigorating being out on my own. I was excited to stay in the seedy motel a couple hours away when I was sent on a travel assignment, and when I got to use my company credit card for lunch, I felt like a big shot.

The work was challenging and never-ending. Turning a pile of notes about a game into a readable and hopefully interesting story is harder than it seems.

I'll never forget my first real compliment at the newspaper. The editor wrote a daily roundup. It was a couple of weeks in, and I made the roundup. The editor highlighted the lede I wrote about a girls' high school soccer match. It was a simple gesture I remember 20 years later.

Working at the newspaper taught me a lot in a short time. I learned what it meant to be on deadline, and I felt a small high each night when I turned in my article for the day. It may not have seemed like much, but completing something tangible that would be out in the world the next day was a rewarding feeling.

To celebrate, I'd head down to the only bar in town to meet up with my new friends, all coworkers at the newspaper, before last call.

As the new guy, I was a slow writer and usually worked right up to deadline. More often than not, they'd have stopped serving drinks by the time I got there. So instead of having a nightcap, I'd become the de facto designated driver.

The hours were long, and I wasn't paid much, but I loved sports, and my hypothesis was that this love would translate to a job that I enjoyed.

The reason I regret leaving my job as a sports reporter wasn't because it ended my time with sports as a focal point in my life.

I'd accepted that I wasn't good enough to be a professional athlete long ago, and it didn't take long to realize that being surrounded by sports was much different than participating in them.

I regret it because the people at the newspaper did their part to make work fun; I still had so much to learn, and I didn't truly give it a chance.

The company culture was good. The team was very welcoming. The old-timers invited me over for dinner, and the younger crew invited me to go fishing, bowling, and snowboarding with them. They made sure to make me feel at home.

The management did a good job explaining the business, and I understood the importance of my work. It was a "dying industry," but they weren't going to give up. They wanted to write compelling stories, and the commitment to their subscribers was authentic. They felt like and acted as guardians of the community.

I got good training, and it was clear who to go to if I had questions.

After I got my assignment for the day, I was given freedom to spend my time as I wanted as long as my story made it in by deadline. I got timely, direct feedback, both good and bad.

The work didn't feel the way I envisioned it would, as Bill Simmons–level fame proved to be more unattainable than I had ever imagined, but it was fun.

However, my work FOMO didn't allow me to see all the good happening around me at the time.

I became solely focused on my pay rate. Instead of taking a deep breath and acknowledging that I was in a cool part of my story, I started to obsess over how much money was being deposited into my bank account every other week.

I didn't need more money, but I was bothered that my friends were making more. If I knew then what I know now, I would have stayed longer and let the things I was learning soak in.

In hindsight, I had more than enough money. With almost no responsibilities other than my $400-per-month furnished apartment, I had no reason to need more than I had at that moment.

And yet, as I scrolled through Facebook, it seemed like my friends were somehow getting further and further ahead of me. I started to worry that I was somehow falling behind on the compensation side of things.

Eventually the Facebook creeping turned into actual conversations. My brother Nick had a job at a huge insurance company at the time and said he could probably get me an interview for an entry-level job where I'd be making four times more money than at the newspaper.

I figured it couldn't hurt to go through the application process, and before I knew it, less than 10 months into my time in Idaho, I was onto something new: something I had very little interest in but that offered a nice salary and good benefits.

I'll never forget my editor's face when I told him I was leaving. At the time, I thought he was disappointed in me, but looking back on it, I think he was sad for me. I'm sure he'd seen dozens of people leave his happy little newspaper for more money and knew the choice rarely led to more contentment.

When I arrived at AIG, the niceties of office life were initially pretty cool. I started drinking coffee for the first time, because it was free and I was bored. The bathrooms had beautiful wood paneling, and I had my own cubicle to decorate as I pleased.

Unlike my newspaper job, the management team didn't take the time to explain why we were doing what we were doing. We never spoke of a purpose, but it felt like the only goal was to maximize profits. I did get swept up in the idea of more responsibilities and envisioned the steps I'd need to take to earn even more money.

Lucky for me, that didn't work out either.

Two years into the job, this time not by choice, I would be changing careers again. The Great Recession was crippling financial institutions across the country, and AIG was at the top of the list.

I was close to the cheapest labor in the building, so when they were forced to cut costs, I kept my job longer than most. I knew I would be fine either way. The extra income was nice, but I had seen firsthand that I could get by on far less.

This wasn't the case for everyone, though. It was painful to watch my coworkers with families relying on each paycheck get let go unexpectedly for no fault of their own.

Insurance is supposed to be a sure thing, a stable industry. So when layoff after layoff decimated our office, it became abundantly clear that "sure things" don't exist.

And if there were truly no sure things, I thought, *why not do something that was more fun?*

A few months later, King of Pops was born.

FOMO pushes us to do more. It can inspire us to get out into the world and live life more fully. However, it also assumes that you aren't already in the right place. We can only be in one place at a time, and once you leave, you're gone.

At any point, you need to be fully present where you are. Having one foot out the door, thinking about your next destination, is a sure path to overlooking all the great things happening around you.

When it comes to work FOMO, the same ideas apply. A desire for more is healthy, but it's unlikely your next job will be inherently better. What most assume requires a new job often can be accomplished right where you are. Great organizations are open to providing new opportunities in areas that interest you.

Maybe you can combine the things you like about your current work with the things that you want to be doing in the future without changing jobs completely. At the very least, you can ask for more.

And when it comes to money—the part of work that we all obsess over—if you do good work, it will come. Changing jobs for more money may be necessary, but I've rarely talked to someone whose new higher-paying job is more fulfilling or fun. I have spoken to people who dug into their organization, created massive value, and were appreciated by people they respected, rewarded with more money, and felt happy with their work.

YOU'LL NEVER HAVE ENOUGH

At the time of writing this book, I'm diving headfirst into my forties. If you look at the stats, my best money-earning years are still ahead of me, with take-home pay peaking for most people between ages 55 and 64.

That's an exciting prospect. Like most people, I can imagine doing things with a larger number in my bank account. And yet, I've gotten comfortable with what I have.

When I got laid off, I knew I could have earned far more money if I found another job in the insurance industry.

During my two-year stint within a corporate juggernaut, I caught a glimpse of what that life could look like for those who stick with it. The company parking lot was littered with luxury cars, and the fantasy football league buy-in certainly didn't seem like "just for fun" to me.

And I'll admit, even as someone writing a book about having fun at work, I feel some type of way each time I come to find out that someone I know is taking home exponentially more money than I am with far less effort.

I currently feel like I have "enough" money, so it may seem easy to preach about this idea now. But I can honestly say I have been able to increase my salary every couple of years, and it doesn't feel a whole lot different. My brother and I have built a business that has increased in value each year, but it doesn't feel any different.

The people happiest in life end up on the idea of "having enough" at some point. And the idea of enough is not about earning a specific number. It's a realization that wealth and happiness are far less related than our ego wants us to think.

If we take a moment to reflect on it, happiness (not money) is what we are all after.

In the early days, out on the cart, King of Pops didn't accept credit cards.

We were always on the move, and mobile payment companies like Square were not quite around yet. That meant if we had a busy day, we would have a stack of cash. In our first year, when my brother Nick and I were the only employees, the big bills would slowly accumulate during the day. A bunch of $2.50 pops would turn into $10, $20, $50 and $100 bills. When we got back to HQ, those bills would be neatly stacked and organized, ready to get deposited at the bank. And the small bills, ones and fives, became "walking-around money."

"Walking-around money" was great for buying burritos, a round of beers, or any unexpected things that might come our way. The thick stack of bills wasn't going to make or break our life, but it made us feel like we were doing something.

To this day, with the proliferation of credit cards and digital payments, I still like to have some "walking-around money," and my wife has adopted this practice as well.

In the book *I Will Teach You to Be Rich*, Ramit Sethi lays out a practical playbook to achieve financial independence. He walks readers through how to approach student debt, negotiate salaries, and even how to face important financial conversations with your significant other.

There are several practical tips in this book that I immediately adopted, but its most valuable idea to me isn't about money; it's about taking the time to think about the things that make us feel good.

Getting a high-end coffee every morning from your favorite barista is not a financially prudent decision. If you got a coffee before work every day for a year, you'd spend well over $1,000. To me, that isn't worth it, but if that is your favorite experience of the day, and you can afford to do it, the fancy coffee is 100% worth it.

He describes these things, both big and small, as "your rich life." And it is something each of us needs to define for ourselves.

Having an unnecessarily thick stack of small bills that I can peel off without thinking twice about it is part of my "rich life."

"Your rich life is not just about money," writes Sethi. "It's about having the freedom to design your life around what matters most to you."

After reading Sethi's book, I took action. I made some practical changes in my finances and thought hard about what my relationship with money was like and how I wanted to use it as a tool. I invested, automated my finances, and started a quarterly financial review with my wife. But I also didn't make everything about money. I had fun with it.

A handful of years later, I stumbled upon another book, *Die with Zero*, written by Bill Perkins. This book, written by another rich guy, took the concept of maximizing our money a step further. If we only save up for retirement, our ability to enjoy that money will be limited by our age and health.

The story in the book that stuck with me was when Bill, early in his career, living crammed in an impossibly small apartment in New York City, was lambasted by his boss for investing a portion of his measly salary when he was barely getting by. While Sethi says "the best time to start investing is 10 years ago, and the second-best time is now," Perkins points out that money doesn't have the same value to us at every point in our life. When he was young, he was one step away from making a lot more money, and the tiny bit that he was able to save wasn't going to make enough difference to justify missing out on the experiences available to him at that time in his life.

It's pretty easy to imagine the excitement of being young and without responsibilities, living in New York City. My instinct would have been to figure out a way to save some money as well, but the point Bill's boss made was about how many more great experiences that money would be able to buy him then.

Even with compounding interest, he would be best served by embracing experiences rather than setting a small amount of a small salary aside.

The concepts in both books are super valuable, and I wish I read them earlier. They help to demystify our relationship with money. I know in my heart there is no magic number for our bank accounts that will make us happy; experiences matter more than money.

Just don't forget that work is one of those experiences that should be valued. Both authors thoughtfully talk about parlaying money, the result of your work, into a life with rich experiences, but they don't address the work itself. It doesn't matter if you're in New York City, New Orleans, or New Mexico, you're going to spend about half of your adult life at work.

There is so much written about optimizing work, reducing work, and managing the money you earn at work. There is even more written about personal fulfillment and being happy.

But it is as if we've given up on the idea of enjoying our work. That isn't OK.

Most days, work will consume about half of your waking hours. Think of it this way: Monday through Friday, if you get eight hours of sleep each night then work for eight hours, there are just eight hours left to do everything else. And that doesn't count getting to work, stressing about work, talking to your loved ones about work, etc.

So many people have come to accept their work life as a means to an end, squirreling away what they can to create experiences later on when they eventually retire.

Lately, I've been daydreaming about taking a trip to Greece. The thought of slurping down fresh seafood while seated outside one of those picturesque, white terra-cotta buildings as I look out over the bright, blue water gets me excited.

Exotic vacations are great, but those experiences are such a small sliver of your time.

Imagine you're eating a meal at a fancy restaurant. Vacations, heck, even retirement are far from the main course. At best, they are the dessert, but for most they are more like the amuse-bouche— French for "palate teaser," the tiny taste of food served before the meal in some fancy restaurants.

Like it or not, for most of your adult life, work is the main course. You'll spend more time doing *work* than anything else.

If the amuse-bouche is amazing but the rest of the meal is terrible, you wouldn't go back to that restaurant ever again.

In the same way, if your work affords you a handful of fun things to do each year, but the work itself is terrible, you shouldn't continue that job.

It just isn't worth it. You want a good meal, not a couple tasty bites.

It's difficult to come to this realization by reading about it alone. It's something you have to feel, get to know, and eventually lean into. You have to be open to it and on the lookout for it.

Money, more than anything else, can make people feel stuck— as if they don't have options and are beholden to work that doesn't serve them.

Happiness, not money, is what we are truly after. Our rush to accumulate wealth is the biggest factor that prevents us from having fun at work. Jumping from job to job for a larger paycheck can be exhilarating, but it doesn't add up to sustained fun and an overall quality of life.

How to Stop Rushing and Start Enjoying

My two-year-old daughter is turning out to be a picky eater.

I'm not a great cook, but I'm efficient in the kitchen. I'm good at quickly throwing together some combination of ingredients that we have in stock for a passable meal. My hasty creations haven't been a problem for me and my wife, but our child can taste the urgency of my cooking.

My mother-in-law, on the other hand, takes her time. She regularly makes us the Jamaican classics—oxtail, brown stew chicken, and jerk pork, to name a few. Each of these meals requires planning. The meat is marinated for long periods of time and carefully cooked to perfection.

Not so surprisingly, my daughter is a better eater when her grandmother's cooking is on offer. Her food is special; she's made many of the same dishes thousands of times, and she learned them from her mom, who has cooked them thousands of times as well.

It's not the type of thing you can get home from work after a long day and throw together. Time is the ingredient that we so often try to skip.

The rest of this book is full of tactics, tips, and tricks to make your work more enjoyable. But before we get to that, it is important to realize that rushing through things is the most common path to unsatisfying work.

Good things take time to develop, and your future self is going to be struggling with the same questions and self-doubt at each step along your journey.

By 2016, we were off to the races with King of Pops. By pushing hard, we were able to quickly expand our business across the South. We had pop kitchens in Charleston, Charlotte, Greenville, and Richmond, with plans to open in Nashville and Savannah.

It seemed like the more effort we put in, the more we got out.

That same year, we bought a 70-acre nursery a 40-minute drive west of Atlanta. With great enthusiasm, we hired a team, spent a lot of money on soil, and patched up the infrastructure.

Our mission was pure. We were committed to supporting local farmers, and we felt a duty to move the conversation on environmental sustainability forward. What better way to do that than through ice pops, right?

So the world's first pop farm, King of Crops, was born. We planned on growing fruit for our pops, composting our waste, and teaching folks about sustainability. I pictured myself riding our tractor through a pristine, bountiful farm in no time.

Fast-forward almost a decade and it's still very much a work in progress. We have acres of established blueberries, muscadines, and blackberries. We've partnered with an amazing business called Compost Now, which has diverted millions of pounds of food waste. And we've made some tasty pops with the fruit we've harvested.

However, it has taken far longer and cost far more than we hoped. On the cart and in the kitchen, we can iterate quickly, but on a farm, you get one season per year. We were used to moving fast and making things happen, but no amount of movement can change the seasons. Spring will come when it is going to come, no matter what you do.

In farming you get one attempt per year to grow your crops. We've gotten it wrong more times than right, but luckily, we aren't on a tight timeline. This is a project that will take a lifetime. If we have a good year selling pops, we can invest. Other times, it gets put on the back burner.

It's worth being aware of which parts of your work can be influenced by additional effort and which require time. Since we can't slow down some parts and speed up others, we've got to figure out a way to enjoy each season.

I happen to believe that, like my mother-in-law's cooking, our work gets better with time, that the layers of meaning that we get from working on the same problem year after year make for a more meaningful existence.

Most people can relate to the idea of projects gaining meaning over time, but research presented in the Work Institute's *2018 Retention Report* indicates that quit rates are increasing nearly every year. We are staying at each stop for shorter and shorter stints.

We have so much more choice in our careers than prior generations had, and while this is a good thing, it can prevent us from fully digging into an opportunity.

Unfortunately, the word *fun* doesn't make its way into much research related to work, but there are numerous studies that correlate higher satisfaction and engagement levels with longer tenure.

For their *2020 Employee Engagement Trends Report*, Quantum Workplace collected turnover information representing over six hundred thousand employees that, unsurprisingly, found a strong correlation between employee turnover and engagement. Disengaged employees are more likely to leave their organization.

However, these studies are almost always considered from a top-down managerial perspective.

The same data would suggest that if you don't want to jump from job to job, figure out a way to increase your engagement.

It's a two-way street. The organization and the individual are both responsible for making the work engaging and fun.

I believe that overall, we'd be happier and have more fun if we stuck with things longer and appreciated the opportunity we found ourselves in right now. That said, I know this path isn't possible for everyone.

Just know that rushing from job to job, stacking experience after experience, with the idea that it is going to somehow add up to something more is not the only path.

This chapter highlights the simplest ways I've found to have fun at work when it comes to career planning. To recap:

1. You'll look back fondly on the tough stuff that you are struggling with right now. Lean into your work, and remember, *these are the good ol' days.*

2. Changing careers is rarely the quickest or surest path to having more fun at work. Put in the effort to make your current work fun before jumping ship.

3. Focusing on how much money you're earning rather than on having fun at work is going to leave you unhappy for a huge chunk of your life. Instead, focus on doing good work, have fun, and the money will come.

Based on where you are in your career, the next steps may look a little different.

When It's Not Up to You

This may seem hard to believe right now, but one day you'll miss the days when you were doing the work instead of directing it. You'll miss the satisfaction of having your hands in the day-to-day activities.

If you're fed up and think it might be time to change jobs, ask yourself these questions:

- Am I having a bad day, month, or longer?

    It's easy to overreact to a bad day. First, make sure your feelings are a result of your work and not something else going on. If it is work-related, keep track of how long the dissatisfaction sticks around. Set aside an amount of time that you're going to wait to see if things get better instead of reacting to the circumstances of one or a few days.

- Have I talked to anyone about how I'm feeling?

    For things to improve, you need to tell someone about it. It is difficult and can be uncomfortable, but it is always better to thoughtfully talk through what is bothering you rather than bottling it up and leaving without a word.

- Are there changes I can make that will improve how I'm feeling?

    This one seems obvious, but sometimes there are changes that are 100% within our control that we can take to make things more fun. Get creative and go for it. If the other option is to leave anyway, what do you have to lose?

- What am I looking for that this work isn't providing?

    Your last step before jumping ship is to identify what is lacking. You certainly can't find something if you don't know what you are looking for. Instead of focusing on what you dislike about your current work, think about what your ideal work would look and feel like. Once you identify it, test and confirm that you aren't able to get at it through your current gig.

One last thing: if you aren't getting paid enough to get by, be sure to ask for what you need before moving on to a new position.

When It's Up to You

If you are building something you believe in, it constantly feels like you are one step away from breaking through—one more project away from all your business-building dreams coming true.

That feeling is what drives you to do amazing work, and it can be both painful and a certain brand of fun at the same time. If you're not careful, over time, it can drive you crazy as well.

Once you complete the project—you know, that one project that is supposed to bring everything together and change the trajectory of your business forever—you'll realize there is actually something else that needs to be done.

And on, and on, and on. This story never ends.

When you are feeling anxious and in a rush to get through the next big thing, ask yourself these questions:

- Am I really going to feel any differently once this is completed?
- Am I taking time to reflect on the team's wins or immediately moving on to the next thing?
- Do we need to grow? And will growing actually contribute to fulfilling our purpose (or our bottom line)?
- Is this hectic, rushing energy serving me and the company or making everyone around me (and myself) miserable?

CHAPTER 3

Ownership Is Free to Take

OUR FAVORITE IDEAS ARE OUR OWN

My childhood revolved around sports, video games, and trying to straddle the line between being a good student and fitting in.

By junior year of high school, I wanted to differentiate myself ever so slightly. I spent my summer playing disc golf, a sport that has continued to grow for decades but remains far from mainstream. And at night, I would log into my computer and play Everquest, an early massively multiplayer online role-playing game.

In both of these worlds, I fairly quickly figured out how to make money while "playing."

If you aren't familiar with disc golf, it is similar to what disc golfers call "ball golf." The goal is to throw a special type of Frisbee, called a disc, from a tee pad toward a basket that has chains to help catch the disc. The fewer throws from the tee pad to the basket, the better.

Instead of tucked-in polo shirts and expensive greens fees, most disc golf courses are free to play, and there is no dress code, although you will see a healthy amount of tie-dye.

The disc golf course closest to my house had a number of ponds scattered throughout the 18 holes. For right-handed players, the normal flight of a Frisbee is fairly predictable. It almost always veers to the left at the end of its flight path. In the Frisbee world, this is called a "hyzer," and it takes time to learn that you typically want to throw your disc not directly at your target but a bit to the right to take into consideration that it will skip back to the left once it touches down.

While this is a simple concept, it's not easy to do, so there were some spots where I had witnessed these ponds take prisoner dozens of discs.

Most discs cost about $10, but finding a store that stocks them can be a challenge. Back then, online shopping wasn't a thing, and most towns didn't have a Frisbee store.

On one particularly hot summer day, after watching my favorite disc splash into the water, I decided to go in after it.

I'd never seen anyone in these ponds. I'm not sure if it was allowed. There weren't any signs posted saying it wasn't, but they probably weren't necessary. The muddy banks and brown water were far from inviting. The ponds were swamp-like, sporting a thin film on top, and if you got too close, there was a certain funk that kept most people away.

Just not me on this day.

I took off my Chaco sandals and gingerly stepped into the water. I was knee-deep in the mud when my toe grazed something that didn't belong there. I reached in hoping to retrieve my prized Frisbee. Sure enough, it was a disc, but it wasn't mine.

I tossed it to the shore and took another step into the water. Every couple of minutes, I would find another disc and toss it ashore.

I must have found 20 that day in less than 30 minutes. Unfortunately, none of them was the one I had just lost. I didn't have a towel, so as I sat there letting the summer sun dry me off, I flipped through the assortment of discs, several of which were brands I'd never seen.

The norm in the disc golf world is to write your name, phone number, and Professional Disc Golf Association number on the back of your discs. If you find someone else's equipment, disc golf code is to try to get it back to them. It's a fringe sport, and the little details like this are what make the community so special. About half of the Frisbees I found had their owners' info on the backs.

So when I got home, I called the numbers, left voicemails, and waited. A week or so later, I was only able to get in touch with two of the 10 people. One said I could just keep the disc, and the other arranged to meet up at the course and play a round.

When we met, he was super grateful and slipped the salvaged disc back into his bag with 20 or so others. In those days, I carried three discs, a putter, a mid-range and a long-range. Lots of my friends played with just one disc, but this guy seemingly had a disc for everything.

He said he had spent as much as $50 on a special run of a disc. The one that I had found hadn't cost him that much, but it was no longer in production and was his favorite mid-range disc. He turned the disc over and showed me the tiny writing that outlined the date and production run on every disc. He explained that no two runs are the same, and the very best players can differentiate from one run to the next.

It turned out this dude (I think it's fair to call him a dude) lived two hours away and had come to the course earlier in the year to play in a tournament.

Up until that point, I hadn't considered that people were this obsessive over their discs. I thought there were a handful of shapes and colors, and if you wanted to spend a few extra bucks, you'd get it in tie-dye. But if this fully baked adult was willing to spend half his day driving to meet up with a random teenager to get a beloved disc back, I could certainly sell the ones I had found.

When the man left to drive home, instead of finishing the round, I went back into the pond to retrieve more discs.

Once a week I'd take a stack of discs and my carefully written notes to the post office, carefully place them in the Priority Mail envelopes and mail them away. I got good reviews for my communication and speed, and I started to obsess over my rating.

As summer came to a close, cooler weather made the trips into the pond less comfortable, and with fewer players out on the course, there weren't as many discs to find. However, I was hooked—nothing was safe from my "Can I sell this on eBay?" mindset.

I sold the things in my room that I hadn't used in a while. I ventured into the depths of our basement and dragged out my parents' old stuff, begging them to let me sell it. And instead of simply playing Everquest, which I had become obsessed with, I teamed up with my friend, who was much better at the game, and sold in-game items like swords, armor, and shields to other players in the online world.

In hindsight, there was nothing particularly fun about being an online retailer. If my parents, a.k.a. my bosses at the time, had told me I had to go search for lost items in a pond, play a computer game in a specific way, or start an eBay store, I certainly would have resisted.

However, because the ideas were my own and I could act on them however and whenever I wanted, they didn't feel like work. I spent time writing catchy headlines, crafting better item descriptions, and capturing more engaging images. I did everything I could to create a positive experience, and when I fell short, I called customers who were unhappy to smooth things over.

I cared a whole lot.

Still, if someone would have asked me at that time if work was fun, I would have said no.

If someone asked me if selling stuff on eBay was fun, I would have said yes.

Freedom at work is much the same. If you're able to inject your own ideas into your day-to-day activities, it will be more fun.

PEOPLE SUPPORT THE IDEAS THEY HELP TO CREATE

Most jobs have a tedium that is hard to avoid. Running King of Pops is no different.

For every hour spent tasting and dreaming up new flavors, there are another 20 hours of chopping, macerating, and blending fruit to make that new flavor a reality.

Take strawberries for example—everyone loves them, and they make some of the most delicious pops. The sweet tanginess of a perfectly ripe strawberry is refreshing, and the soft fruit is much more satisfying than the watery innards of its blueberry or blackberry brethren.

The denser texture in a strawberry leads to pops that are more substantial when you bite into them and make the perfect canvas to introduce other more novel flavors like hibiscus, basil, or balsamic.

We've made dozens of strawberry flavors, including our best-selling fruit pop, Strawberry Lemonade.

But before a strawberry can be blended and made into a pop, you have to "top it," which means removing the green leaves that adorn the top of each one. There are countless tools and strategies to do this efficiently, but there is no escaping this mind-numbing task if you have hundreds of pounds of strawberries to prep.

It's not a glamorous job, but those hours feel different when the flavor idea is your own and you're working toward something you believe in.

Work is just more fun if you're part of the creation process.

There is no telling how many flavors we've developed at King of Pops. We stopped counting at five hundred, and we've just been saying "over five hundred" for years now.

Some of our flavors are straightforward, like Blueberry Lemonade or Fresh Peach. Others are more adventurous, like Pineapple Habanero, Strawberry Tomato with Georgia Olive Oil, or Grapefruit Fennel (yuck).

I chuckle to myself when people say "That would make a good pop flavor," because the truth is, most things that taste good will make a good pop flavor. And this fact leads to a lot of new flavors.

The constant innovation is a lot of fun, and it's a big reason people keep coming back to try our pops. It's fun to seek out the latest creations on the cart and strike up a conversation with the pop slinger about their thoughts on the menu that day.

In our early days, everyone on our small team wore multiple hats. There was an ongoing conversation about each and every facet of the business. We'd take turns doing computer work at a small desk in the production area. If it was your turn to rest your legs and do some admin work at the desk, you couldn't go far because every 10 minutes or so we'd need an extra set of hands.

Between emails you'd be tasting new pop bases, giving feedback on sweetness, acidity, texture, and balance. And then when a batch was frozen, you'd stop what you were doing, wash your hands, and help to get things packaged as quickly as possible so they wouldn't melt.

The entire crew would be in the kitchen making pops one day and out selling on the cart the next. And you can be sure if someone came up with a new flavor the day before, they were preaching the greatness of their creation to anyone who would listen once they were in front of potential customers.

The creator didn't get anything if their pop sold well, other than the satisfaction that they'd made something people liked, and that was enough.

We were all part of the flavor creation process. Even those who weren't coming up with new flavors seemed bought in. Just by being in the room, we all felt more invested in the product.

Engagement is not something you need to be sneaky about. There is nothing manipulative about being enthusiastic. Customers and employees alike get swept up in the excitement when something is new and they are among the first to try it.

The truth is, although we've made hundreds of new creations, most of our sales come from a handful of our most traditional flavors. Nearly every cart will have Chocolate Sea Salt, Strawberry Lemonade, Mango Tangerine, and Cookies 'n Cream because they are beloved by so many.

At this point, it would be a lot easier to make the same seven or eight flavors every day. And you could make the case that this would be the best path for increasing our profitability, but how much fun would that be?

I never really thought about it until I was writing this book, but a big part of our quest for new delicious flavors is truly a quest to have fun together.

Our production team, lovingly referred to as the Frosty Freaks, is constantly engaging others with its latest work. If you spend a day or two at our HQ in Atlanta, you'll more than likely see a dish bin full of pops on offer. A proud creator will walk through the office, handing out their latest pop iteration, getting feedback, and sharing something delicious. There are Ziploc bags with handwritten notes labeling the version number and a few words about the iterations—"more salt," "less citrus," "sweetened with honey instead of agave," etc.

Using a sample pop as a metaphor for engagement may not seem completely transferrable to most other work scenarios, but in many ways, it is.

When you get your sample pop, there are no instructions on what to do next, and typically one of two things happen.

1. Say thanks, and get back to work.
2. Ask the creator questions about the pop, and let them know your thoughts about how it could be improved.

To be engaged at work, we need to be in an engaging environment. Each of us has a responsibility to figure out how to make our workplace more fun.

It would be nice if the work at King of Pops was as straightforward as making a delicious product, but that is just the beginning.

We have a small fleet of used pickup trucks to get King of Pops carts from point A to point B. They are absolutely essential for the business to operate.

And yet, they are almost always neglected.

One day, instead of focusing on a new pop flavor, a fairly new employee named Justin walked up to me to share a stack of five clipboards with a simple table printed on each.

Without being asked, Justin had created a basic truck maintenance log and spent a couple of hours going through our current trucks to get the first column updated with the most recent info.

He asked if he could be responsible for maintaining the trucks. He proposed that we pay him instead of the mechanic to do the basics like oil changes, windshield wiper replacement, and other simple fixes that were in his wheelhouse. And when the truck needed to go into the shop, he'd manage that process, logging and verifying that the work was done.

I was ecstatic. If this had been a pop flavor, it would have been Banana Puddin'—my all-time favorite.

For the next year, it seemed like our trucks didn't age. The fleet was in great shape, and that meant we were late to fewer events, pop slingers had less stress, and the AC actually blew cold air to provide a moment of solace from the extreme Atlanta heat.

Unfortunately, when Justin left to pursue a career in marketing, the truck checklists fell by the wayside.

We tried our best to assign the task to someone else. We found someone who liked cars, clearly laid out the expectations, and handed him Justin's old clipboards, but it was never the same because we didn't encourage the new truck maintenance owner to make it his own.

A decade or so later, I was catching up with Justin. It was in the middle of another heat spell in Georgia and like clockwork the freezers were having a hard time keeping up. I was complaining about the never-ending struggles of refrigeration maintenance and how much I resisted this part of my job.

To my surprise, he was nodding his head, commiserating with the ongoing struggle.

This didn't align with the picture in my head of the happy-go-lucky guy who, out of the blue, wanted to keep our pickup trucks in good working order.

I asked him why he had offered to help us with the trucks all those years ago, and his answer was simple and profound.

"It's just more fun when you take ownership of something, and it needed to be done," he said.

Putting yourself out there and taking some type of risk is an important ingredient in creating fun at work. In every organization, you're going to be judged on the work that you do. It might as well be your ideas that you're judged on.

WE ARE TOLD WORK IS A SACRIFICE

I got the perfect attendance award every year in elementary school. They should have given this award to my mom, because I didn't have much of a choice. Monday through Friday, there was a flow in our household that was not to be disrupted.

The first day of school I ever missed was in middle school. I was pretty sad after our childhood dog, Maggie, passed away.

Maggie was a Scottish terrier, and my mom grew up with a Scottish terrier named Andy. For whatever reason, this was the only breed of dog our family considered. They aren't super common, and when my mom found a litter of puppies in South Georgia, she broke from her firm midwestern discipline and agreed to let me come along on a weekday.

It felt wrong heading onto the interstate as school buses passed going the other direction. When we arrived, I remember approaching a pickup truck with a large cage in the back. I expected to see a handful of cute playful dogs, but by the time we arrived, there was only one skittish puppy remaining. The dog had a strong aversion to us, and when her owners walked to the truck to try and coax her out, she backed up even further into the corner.

Against our better judgment, we decided she was the dog for us. Her parents, Barbie and Twig, watched as we pulled away, and I sat in the backseat with our new dog as she yelped uncontrollably, clearly not wanting to go anywhere with us.

She turned out to be a unique, lovable dog, and we had a lot of good times together, but that isn't the point. I don't remember any other days in sixth grade. That day was memorable because it was the exception.

As if you need to be reminded, the everyday march our society subscribes to is as follows:

- Work hard in school to get into college.
- Work hard in college to get a good job.
- Work hard at your job to get promoted.
- Keep working hard as long as possible so you don't run out of money in retirement.

There has always been an undercurrent resisting these ideals, but most of those conversations revolve around less work. And while I'm neither for nor against less work, I'm frustrated that somehow we've neglected to spend much time thinking about how to make work more fun.

It is pretty easy to feel like this one-size-fits-all approach does not fit for you. These patterns run deep, and it may not feel like you have a choice in the matter, but the truth is that you do. You can make your work more fun if you're able to take ownership of it.

But it's not the type of ownership that shows up on tax returns and shares of equity that matters here. I owned a tiny amount of AIG stock when I worked there. I technically had some ownership stake in the company, but that didn't create a feeling of ownership.

The nontechnical type of ownership I'm convinced is required to have more fun at work is something that any one of us can take, no matter where we work, at any time.

Once you work in this way, there is no going back. You feel free.

My path to freedom involved starting my own business. And it could be the best option for you. Entrepreneurship is a beautiful dance, but it's a dance that more often than not is you alone on the dance floor trying something new, with everyone else safely against the wall, their backs turned ever so slightly, trying their best to avoid eye contact.

It's a dance that also doesn't pay so great most of the time.

And while being your own boss leaves it 100% up to you to create freedom, plenty of my business-owning peers have unintentionally created the same "work for work's sake" circumstances that they were trying to avoid in the first place by starting their own thing.

Great employers go out of their way to encourage their employees to take ownership. Unfortunately, most employers are not "great." When you feel like you're being treated like a cog in the wheel, you have three options: keep being a cog, leave, or do something about it.

If you decide to live with it, you're selling yourself short.

If you're going to leave, there is a high likelihood that the next place won't be much different.

So, much like we outlined in the last chapter, you might as well do your best to take ownership where you are now.

THERE IS NO GOING BACK

We've had hundreds of employees come and go. A few were laid off when times were tough, some were let go for performance reasons, but most others left when they felt ready.

For a while, I couldn't figure out why this was happening. I selfishly wanted to make it stop. When a coworker is taking ownership and having fun at work, it makes your work more fun too. And when they leave, it stings.

More than anything else, the employees that thrive the most at our company see firsthand how surprisingly simple starting something new can be. Once you've been around to watch it for a while, that feeling starts to rub off on you.

A couple years after we started, we realized it would probably be smart if we were able to make some money in the winter, when people weren't buying as many pops. We quickly landed on Christmas tree delivery. People buy Christmas trees in the winter, and we had a bunch of pickup trucks just sitting around without the need to transport King of Pops carts.

To make it more fun, we delivered the trees while wearing elf garb and referred to each other by our self-appointed elf names. I'd answer the phone by saying, "Taco the Elf, how can I help you?"

A few seasons in, this business achieved its goal. It allowed our seasonal employees to get paid longer and justified the payroll of more salaried employees.

It did something else too. If you saw how easy it was, from ideation to implementation, you couldn't help but think about your own business idea. An above-average number of King of Pops alumni have started their own businesses, from pet sitting to social media coaching to fractional HR. And when people leave to work for another organization, they are more likely to take ownership of the work they do there.

Don't sell yourself short. Don't fall into the trap of thinking other people's ideas are better than your own just because they said them out loud. Taking ownership and having fun require putting your neck on the line. If your idea goes well, that is amazing. If it doesn't, it turns out that failure isn't really that bad of an outcome.

It's always better to stumble and fall trying to do something great than sit idly in the background.

How to Take Ownership at Work

It isn't hard to know when you're taking ownership of work. You'll know when you're excited to go to work. When you have to remind yourself to head home for dinner and resist jumping into a work project that can wait on the weekend. When there is something you want to do, and nobody is going to know if you do or don't do it, but you do it anyway.

Once you begin to see work as an opportunity to contribute, everything changes. It's important that this isn't a tactic. If your goal is to earn more freedom in order to sneak off and waste time on your phone, you're missing the point. And it probably won't end well.

Waiting to get told what to do is compliance.

Doing great work because it is what you want to do is taking ownership, and it is fun. This frame of mind isn't just for owners. It's 100% in your control, and if you are able to embrace it, you will find yourself enjoying more freedom and having more fun.

When we don't take ownership of our work, we are stuck thinking about freedom in terms of work hours. But having fun at work is really about autonomy.

In 1985, psychologists Edward Deci and Richard Ryan created an analysis of human motivation called the Self-Determination Theory. In it they hypothesized that autonomy is key to intrinsic satisfaction.

Their work has influenced how experts approach several facets of our life—teaching, coaching, parenting, and, yes, work.

If you pay attention, smart companies are finding ways to inject more autonomy into their culture.

At Patagonia they have a famous policy—"Let my people go surfing"—that empowers employees to leave work to "catch a good swell, go bouldering for an afternoon, pursue an education, or get home in time to greet the kids when they come down from the school bus."

To take advantage of this, employees just have to get their work done.

In 2014, Zappos adopted Holocracy, a method of decentralized management and organizational governance, which claims to distribute authority and decision-making.

Zappos's website explains, "At Zappos, everybody is given the keys to drive the company forward. In most companies, new ideas have to be approved by a manager or a chain of managers. As a company that uses a self-managed organizational structure, we encourage Zapponians to identify areas of opportunity within the organization and propose solutions."

A good workplace can create an environment ripe for autonomy and ownership, but it's ultimately an opportunity each employee must seize. You are the only one who can assign your work meaning, thus it is your responsibility to figure out how to find it.

That might seem a bit intimidating, but it doesn't have to be. Here's how to get started on your path to experiencing more freedom at work.

When It's Not Up to You

Early in your career, as you are learning how you can add the most value, it can be tough to find out how, where, and when to bring your ideas to the table.

The most important step is to ask.

If you feel stuck, try following these steps with your boss:

- Identify a lingering problem you've observed (ideally one that others have acknowledged) that, if improved, will help the company.
- Write a sentence defining the problem and three to five steps you think would begin to solve the problem.
- Ask someone to take a look at your idea (a family member or good friend is best here).
- Sit down with your manager and review your plan. Get feedback and make adjustments.
- Execute.

Leadership may initially be skeptical. Change can be scary for a manager, but don't be discouraged. Many managers are justifiably fearful of wasting time. If this is the case for you, pick one of the steps from your plan that won't take long or impact other team members, and ask if you can get started by doing that one small step and checking back in.

More often than not, once you demonstrate your pure intentions, the rest will fall into place.

When It's Up to You

If you're a decision-maker, the path to creating ownership and freedom for yourself is more straightforward. There may be some nonnegotiables, but by and large, once you're in charge of your schedule, you should set it in a way that works for you.

I recommend setting constraints. Plan to work a certain schedule.

If you work on something until your eyes glaze over for too long, even if you love it, it will stop being fun. If you schedule yourself to work slightly less than you want to, it will leave you with that "pumped up to go to work" feeling that is crucial for having fun at work. If you're living the startup life, and your work requires your undivided attention, allocate a set of hours each week for different types of work to keep things fresh. Working without a schedule might seem like the ultimate freedom, but it can make projects seem more daunting.

If you're a manager trying to get your team to embrace autonomy and create a more fun workplace, start asking more questions. Try the following:

- What do you think the biggest problem or opportunity is right now?
- How would you approach this?
- What do you need to get started?

After you ask those questions, just stay quiet. Resist the urge to fill the silence with more of your fantastic ideas.

Remember, it's best for all parties if the person doing the work feels ownership over it. Your team may look at you funny the first few times you utter these words, but if you stick with it, your team will start to have more fun. And if you get excited about their work, this fun only gets amplified.

CHAPTER 4

Pride Compounds Over Time

YOU HAVE TO CARE FIRST

In 2009, I set out to open the first King of Pops location.

It is a bit disingenuous to say the "first," as I had not considered there would ever be more than one.

By the time I was officially unemployed, it was August. With cooler weather a couple months away, I gave myself a deadline of the following spring—April 1, 2010, to be exact—to be officially open. Lucky for me, I did not define what *open* meant. My confidence as an aspiring entrepreneur was teetering, but I promised myself that I'd give it a go for at least a year, then I could reassess the situation.

At this point in time, the most fun part of the business was watching people's reactions as I explained with a straight face that I was diving headfirst into building an ice pop business. The lack of a true business plan did not stop me from proudly proclaiming to anyone who would listen that King of Pops would be open in the spring.

I'm not much of a backup-plan guy. When I was applying to college, I only applied to the University of Georgia. Luckily, it worked out. This time around, my one and only plan was to open a small shop in a vacant building next to Buddy's gas station, a heavily trafficked slice of an intown neighborhood called Poncey-Highland that I passed through daily.

The space was about six hundred square feet and had been the original checkout, from a time when gas stations were more focused on selling gas than being convenience stores. It was detached from the updated store and positioned awkwardly close to the gas pumps.

It was a weird idea, but in my mind it all made sense. It was a vibrant, cool area, and I felt like over time this could become an unexpected detail the neighborhood would embrace. Plus it had been vacant for years, so I figured I could afford it.

When it came to commercial real estate, I had no idea what I was talking about. With my April 1 deadline looming, I built up the courage to ask the guy at the register if I could talk to the owner. I expected him to hand me a card or something, but instead he walked me down a small hall into a tiny office where one of the owners, Imad, was sifting through a pile of papers.

I told him about my plan for a small shop and asked if he'd be willing to rent me the unused space. He seemed, at the very least, amused. We exchanged numbers, and he agreed to be in touch a couple days later, once he had time to talk to his partners about it.

Weeks passed. I called every day or two. Some days he picked up, other days it went to voicemail. He was never rude, but this clearly wasn't a priority. Still, I pushed on, and eventually they came back with a proposal.

They'd handle the permitting and get the space up to code but also use half the space for a small pizza shop. This was far from ideal, but at this point in time, it was mid-January and my April deadline was fast approaching. So I agreed.

Prior to getting laid off, I had managed to save $7,000. I didn't want to go into debt but planned on using every last dollar to get things up and running. While the gas station people were working on properly permitting the space, I commissioned a friend with beer and the promise of future pops to help me paint a King of Pops mural on the neighboring laundromat wall.

Michael Jackson, the "King of Pop," had died the previous summer, and if painting a gigantic red popsicle on the side of a building in the middle of the winter was not strange enough, when my friend and I painted the words *King of Pops* on the wall, the neighbors were fully intrigued.

Unsure if this was some sort of strange homage to Jackson, art, or a new business, the neighbors looked on with a healthy amount of skepticism and confusion.

The mural we were painting to fill time ended up being an unintentionally masterful marketing effort. Neighbors were looking forward to spring, and as they walked by each day, I was able to start building hype about the business I would be opening.

Having these conversations helped me form and clarify thoughts about the business that I had never considered before.

By the time we finished the mural, a month had passed. During that time, I'd looked over my shoulder regularly, hoping to see activity or construction of some sort happening, but the gas station owners had made little progress on their permitting efforts, and the shop had not been touched. Still, I held out hope.

I worked on recipes, commissioned another friend with beer and the promise of future pops to design a logo, and spent $6,000, nearly everything I had, on a machine from Brazil that was supposed to freeze 88 pops in 30 minutes.

As February came to a close, I took samples of my product to get external feedback. First at a kindergarten class then at Spanx, the women's shapewear company—an excruciatingly intimidating experience that I somehow survived.

By mid-March, I had a brand, look, feel, and several recipes but still nowhere to sell the pops. In a panic, still 100% committed to hitting my self-imposed deadline, I asked the gas station owners if I could sell out of a pushcart in their parking lot until the space was ready. They agreed, and I jumped into action.

I lucked into a shared kitchen that had space for me about a mile away. I went down to city hall to get a business license. I found a classic pushcart from a *paleta* company that had gone bust in Texas. I bought some plywood boards from Home Depot and painted them with chalkboard paint for my menu. And I found a small green umbrella to affix to my cart to help keep it cool.

On April 1, 2010, I pushed the cart from my shared kitchen to the gas station corner, wrote my flavors for the day on my handmade chalkboard, posted my menu and location on Twitter, and considered myself open for business.

It was a relief to be open, and although most of the hundreds of people I'd proclaimed my self-imposed deadline to had no idea I was open, I was proud that I hadn't let them down.

Internal pride manifests itself through holding yourself accountable. You can't expect anyone else to care about your goals if you don't care yourself.

That first King of Pops spot was far from perfect, but I was open. And to my surprise, the cart business I had stumbled upon was quickly gaining traction. Something about the smallness of the cart, the largeness of me, and the quirkiness of the flavors, mural, and everything else stood out.

On Saturdays, people would drive from across the metro area and line up to buy pops. The tiny cart started to get a lot of attention. First locally, then in July CNN ran a story, "Turning lemons into frozen lemonade," highlighting King of Pops' success in light of the financial crisis I had been a victim of the previous year.*

Fifteen years and millions of pops later, the gas station space I had obsessed over remains vacant.

Our pride compels us to do great things. Each time I told someone of my April 1 deadline, the stakes increased. Something they probably didn't remember me speaking of was a commitment that I did not want to break. The commitment was 100% internal, but it was powerful to me.

We assume it is the outside world that determines when we fall short and when we succeed. The reality is that *we* decide.

I have a fiddle-leaf fig tree named Rocky. After losing all its leaves, it was exiled by my wife to the garage. Unwilling to admit

* "CNN: From AIG to 'King of Pops,'" YouTube, January 16, 2013, www.youtube.com/watch?v=3tMPtsqQ3Vk.

defeat, I continued to water it occasionally for months. Six years later, Rocky is thriving proudly in our bedroom.

In life we decide when we've had enough, and we are the only ones who can decide we've failed.

If we don't give up, we can't fail. There is a way to ensure your own success.

Never give up.

PRIDE IS INCONVENIENT

One of the most common questions I get asked is, "How did you learn how to make pops?" People ask in a way that makes it seem like the process must be complicated, but millions of kids of all ages make ice pops in their freezers every summer with little to no instruction.

The truth is, ice pops, like most things in life, are simple. We've been making them for over 15 years, and many of our best ones have only three to five ingredients. Those ingredients are mixed together and frozen.

However, *simple* and *easy* are not the same thing. Although the words are often used interchangeably, they have very little in common.

Something is simple if it lacks complexity.

Something is easy if it takes little effort.

So when people ask how we learned to make them, I tend to avoid the question. I could say we mix some fruit together and freeze it, but that might come off as a bit sassy. Instead, I tell them about our inspiration, the *paleta*.

The Popsicle most of us have grown up with in the United States is made with processed sugar, food coloring, and stabilizers.

The formula was developed for a grocery store, to have a long shelf life and not melt in your trunk en route to your home freezer. It's an inexpensive treat made for the masses.

The *paleta*, on the other hand, is made with fresh, whole ingredients, and you can taste the difference. The two are similar in form. Both *paletas* and Popsicles are sweet frozen liquid on a wooden stick, but the similarities stop there.

There are several generations of artisans in Latin America that have been using straightforward techniques to combine delicious ingredients in a simple way.

When you see a glass case full of *paletas*, it jumps out at you and draws you in. The small imperfections on each bar indicate their handmade nature, and when you taste a good *paleta*, the quality of the ingredients is impossible to ignore.

I'll never forget my first attempt to recreate this magic.

I took a trip to the Dekalb Farmers Market, a one-of-a-kind store just outside of Atlanta that sells amazing food from around the world. The variety and quality draws foodies, restaurateurs, and immigrants who can't find food from their home countries anywhere else.

I filled my cart with loads of beautiful fruit, baked desserts, and different types of dairy. I tried my best to imagine the varieties of flavors from the *paleta* cases so I could take a stab at recreating them.

I returned home and got to work breaking down, chopping, and tasting fruit, and eventually blending things together, crossing my fingers that the tastes would combine in a pleasant way.

I must have made 20 or so flavors that day, with several iterations of each flavor neatly labeled in medicine cups. I used the underside of an art canvas to hold the future *paleta* samples because it fit perfectly in my condo's freezer.

We still make some of those first flavors today. Our first iterations of Chocolate Sea Salt, Pineapple Habanero, Blackberry Ginger Lemonade, and Strawberries 'n Cream were born in my condo with very little fanfare.

I learned an important lesson that first day of testing, one that inspired our brand and how we innovate today. If you combine delicious ingredients, the final product will often be delicious as well.

A good peach is my favorite fruit. Being from Georgia, I've had plenty of amazing ones. But the truth is, no two peaches are the same. If it's a really rainy year, the peach will lack flavor, and when there isn't enough rain, it'll become dry and mealy.

A single peach farm will have a handful of varieties ready for harvest at differing times throughout the summer. Each variety has a different taste profile. In addition, some varieties are freestones, meaning the pit easily separates from the fruit, while others are clingers, where the pit is connected to the fruit, making the process of cutting them up exponentially more difficult.

Peaches are my favorite fruit, but I don't bother buying them for most of the year. To me the standard grocery store "yellow peach" is hardly the same fruit as a ripe peach.

A good peach is juicy and soft but not bruised. It is sweet and tart with a hint of brightness.

Finding one delicious and perfectly ripe peach can be tricky, but when you need one thousand pounds every week, the difficulty level increases dramatically.

The hard work—and the art—is in the sourcing.

You can't cut corners, and quality ingredients are going to cost more. It is why you can buy an eight-pack of Popsicle brand pops at the grocery store for the same price as a single King of Pops pop.

My love of a good peach compels me to make a great peach pop. I will admit, I hold it to a higher standard. I want others to see the light and recognize the greatness of a locally grown, in-season, perfectly ripe peach.

As ridiculous as it may sound, I want to honor the peach.

Pride is inconvenient in this way.

It compels us to do things that make our lives more difficult, like cutting your lawn in perfectly straight lines and making your bed every morning even if nobody else is going to see it. When you look back on it, completing these tasks feels good, and the extra effort is worth it.

Pride is illogical.

It urges us to carry in a trunk full of groceries in one trip, to reject a college because it is a rival of the one you grew up cheering for, or in my case, to refuse Oscar Meyer hot dogs because my dad sold Hormel hot dogs throughout his career. The tangled web of motivations in our brain is unique to each of us and won't always make sense to the outside world.

But most of all, pride is important.

It gives meaning to the mundane and allows for the extra steps required to make a truly special peach pop worthwhile. It allows for our work to be meaningful to us, and that meaning is the only way for work to be fun for an extended period.

What we choose to take pride in is a personal decision.

At King of Pops, we decided early on that instead of growing as big as we could, we would not grow beyond the South. We felt that if we focused on being a regional brand, we would be better positioned to be a positive influence in the local food scene. We'd be able to support more local farms and build more authentic community connections.

I'm super proud of this idea to stay small, but there are people at King of Pops with whom the idea doesn't resonate.

There may be times when the place where you work is operating in a way that goes against your morals. This can make taking pride in your work much more difficult.

If you take great pride in organic farming, then working for Monsanto, which manufactures GMOs and herbicides like Roundup, might be a challenge.

If you have a loved one who has had health issues because of tobacco usage, Philip Morris is a company that could be difficult to work for.

And if you think climate change and recycling are a hoax, you probably won't be drawn to work at Patagonia.

When the work a company does is misaligned with your ideals, in order to take pride in your work, you can look for ways to make an impact that aligns with your values inside the organization. Or you can leave.

It is important to be realistic about your company's mission aligning with your personal ideals, as they are typically not as clear as the examples listed above.

Most employees at King of Pops did not arrive as passionate local farming advocates and probably didn't care more than the average Joe about creating authentic community connections. At the same time, these concepts are not polarizing, meaning they most likely do not exclude the things others might take pride in.

I find this to often be the case.

Unless you are the founder of or planning to start a company, it is unlikely the work will have pride built in from day one. However, that isn't a bad thing.

Great companies inspire employees to align with their mission, and great employees bring their passions into their work and change the trajectory of their company.

When we decide to relentlessly make each other better, the result is a win-win. There is no other way to say it . . . work is fun.

WEAR THE SHIRT

Steve Jobs famously wore a black mock turtleneck, Levi's 501 jeans, and New Balance 991 sneakers nearly every day. He claimed that by having a uniform, he needed to make one less decision each day, allowing him to direct his decision-making energy to more important things.

I wear a King of Pops T-shirt every day.

Unfortunately, other than having a uniform and sharing a first name, our similarities stop there.

At first I was wearing King of Pops shirts every day out of convenience. I wanted to be prepared in case I had to hop on a cart and work a last-minute event.

One day I read the story about Jobs, realized I was already kind of doing it, and decided to lean into the idea of making one less decision each day. So for the last 15 years, unless it's a special occasion, I wear a King of Pops shirt.

I was wearing a King of Pops shirt when my daughter was born, when my wife and I bought a house together, and at my 20-year high school reunion. I wear a red King of Pops shirt on University of Georgia game days, a green one on St. Patrick's Day, and a red, white, and blue one on the Fourth of July.

I have a stack of 50 or so shirts in my rotation. Tuesdays are for tie-dye, but every other day I just pick one from the top of the pile.

What started as a means to simplify things has made a big difference in my life and the trajectory of our company. It's hard to say if I've spared myself from decision fatigue as a result, but it has acted as a recurring litmus test for how I'm feeling about the work I am doing.

If I felt ashamed of the work I was doing, it would be a burden to walk out into the world wearing yet another King of Pops shirt. On the flip side, if the work is meaningful to me, the shirt feels like it is right where it belongs.

I'm constantly surprised when I'm walking through the airport in a city hundreds of miles from the nearest King of Pops cart and someone stops me to say they love our company. That external recognition feels great.

However, the biggest impact of my wardrobe decision has happened internally. If I'm going to wear a King of Pops shirt every day, I want to make damn sure that I'm proud of the work we are doing. I have to believe the work our team is doing is making the world a better place.

I know this impacts my unconscious decisions. When we are developing a new flavor, sending out a marketing email, or handling a customer complaint, I'm aware these decisions are a reflection on me.

We've tried to bottle up this idea and share it with our team. "Wear the shirt" is now one of our core values.

And even though it seems very prescriptive, you don't have to physically display a King of Pops logo to "wear the shirt." The idea is for your work to be more than just a job. The hope is that each of us finds ways to incorporate the things that we find important into our work.

This doesn't happen automatically. Day one, it's just another job. For a new employee, as we review our core values, they are empty words. No matter how emphatically you say them, no matter how much pizzaz you try to put into a slide deck, they are just words.

The goal is for them to become more than just words. A successful company orientation lays the groundwork for what is to come.

When we go over our core values, we make it clear that these ideals were not plucked from thin air but inspired by the experiences of former employees. A group of us took the time to identify the characteristics of the employees that best represented what we are doing and developed the core values accordingly.

When we were building our core values, we brought together a committee of 10 people from different departments across the company. Our then marketing director, who is from Brazil, shared a popular Portuguese phrase: *vestir a camisa*.

The literal translation is to "wear the shirt," but in Brazil the phrase more often means to fully commit to something. In the United States, we see this quite a bit in sports. We all know someone that gets quite fanatical about their team. College football in the South, in particular, seems to embody the "wear the shirt" spirit. People have a school that they care a lot about, and on Saturdays in the fall, the college football spirit is on full display.

For better or worse, you commit to your team. When they have a great season, you are riding a high. My University of Georgia team has been winning a lot recently, taking home the 2022 and 2023 College Football Playoff National Championships.

But wearing the shirt isn't about the result.

My parents both went to the University of Nebraska. The once-great team has not had much success over the last two decades, but my parents still watch every minute of every game, flying back to see one or two games in person each year. Despite poor results, the Nebraska Cornhuskers always show up. They have sold out every game for over 60 years. Win or lose, the fans take pride in showing up, and they have a tradition of clapping for their opponents at the end of the game as a sign of mutual respect.

Japan has not yet had much success on the international soccer stage, but their fans, nicknamed the "Samurai Blue," make headlines each World Cup when spotted picking up trash in the stadium after the game. Many fans bring their own trash bags to the game for this purpose alone.

The games are really just a backdrop for a community to come together.

When other people are committed to something, it makes it easier to commit yourself. There is a snowball of support that leads to more and more pride. It might not seem like clapping after a loss or picking up trash is any fun, but it is.

As humans, it feels good to be part of the community, and that connection helps to incubate pride. In the work world, leaders play a particularly important role in fostering this sense of community. They are among the very first connections a new hire will have. If it is a positive one, it will help to facilitate more and more positive connections. Ideally, these positive connections grow and multiply.

Over time, those connections add up to a general sense of pride in the organization as a whole.

Our relationship with work is similar in many ways to any other relationship we have in life. It can't be forced, and it takes energy from both sides to make it work.

A personal investment is a prerequisite for sustained fun at work.

When we are wrapping up the core values section of our orientation, we always save "wear the shirt" for last. I explain to the new employees that on their first day, this company cannot mean that much to them. It's just a job, after all.

However, if we are doing our part, and they are leaning in as well, it should mean something to them before too long.

Pride is not a singular responsibility. It is up to the company and the individual to come together and create it.

THE ANTI-COUCH POTATO

My brother Nick and I wore ourselves down physically and mentally those first few King of Pops seasons.

We are fairly skinny guys already, but every season we would lose an additional 10 to 15 pounds. We called it "summer weight." It wasn't a good look—more of an emaciated one—and our mom would worry.

We didn't get many breaks. Producing pops meant breaking down fruit, blending, and packaging. And as soon as that was complete, we'd be out somewhere slinging pops—pushing the cart to a spot, getting everything set up, then enthusiastically engaging with customers.

We'd be on our feet all day trying to keep up.

Our normal pace felt so hectic that we looked forward to "drive time," which simply constituted an event that was more than 15 minutes away, enabling rest without the guilt of putting off other work.

Days off were uncommon, and the idea of taking a true break and getting out of town was incomprehensible.

I know this doesn't sound like much fun, but somehow it was.

I felt more alive than I ever had before. I was getting so much done and had so much more to do. We knew we were building something special.

Exhaustion and overload are the stories I find myself pointing to most often when I talk about the early days. On a normal day, we'd take a gallon of water with us, drink it all, and not have to use the restroom because we would sweat it out.

Stories of excessively hard work are the go-to when entrepreneurs reflect on their journey.

However, it is the undercurrent of pride that enables us to put in this type of effort. A stranger cannot fully appreciate why we take pride in what we do, but internally, it is what allows us to push through discomfort.

Over time, pride compounds. It stacks up as different areas of your life blend together. My brother being my business partner added a different element of pride because I didn't want to let him down.

It would be nice if allocating pride was a simple process, if we could fill out a form and suddenly have pride in all the right things. I'd like to take more pride in folding my laundry, cleaning out my car, and pulling weeds in my yard. But pride evolves from meaning. Until you figure out how to find value for yourself in it, pride will be missing.

There are things we can do to stack the deck if we want to manufacture more meaning in our day-to-day lives, like thinking intentionally about the people we're around and the story we want to write, but it takes time for pride to evolve. Pride is not a finite resource, but it doesn't come with an on/off switch either.

When I was growing up, my mom regularly prodded me not to be a "couch potato." The couch potato my mom was referring to is mostly checked out, taking pride in far less than someone who is actively engaging with the world. The more things you touch, the more you learn, the more you'll care about.

The same is true at work. The task-evader won't have nearly as much pride as the go-getter.

Pride comes to us when we put ourselves out there and connect with our work through doing.

Seth Godin makes this point in his book *Linchpin*: "The only purpose of starting is to finish, and while the projects we do are never really finished, they must ship. Shipping means hitting the publish button on your blog, showing a presentation to the sales team, answering the phone, selling the muffins, and sending out your references. Shipping is the collision between your work and the outside world." We decide the story we are going to live and what we are going to put out into the world.

The more you ship, the more pride you take in your work, the more fun you'll have.

How to Start Taking Pride in Your Work

While pride is contagious, it can't be delegated to you or assigned to others.

There is a perception that work motives live on the extremes. You're either in it for the money, or an idealist sacrificing for a cause.

Many wrongly assume that pride in your work is reserved for the idealists, and that those who are in it for the money get their satisfaction from increasing their earnings. But organizations of every type are doing valuable work—work worth caring about, and work that needs your fingerprints.

You can stubbornly resist taking pride in your work, or you can be open to it. You can work hard on finding ways to avoid the work, or you can work hard on the work itself.

This mindset decision starts on day one. Are you leaning forward in your seat and asking questions during orientation, or are you eagerly waiting for it to end?

There are plenty of people whose mindset going in is to avoid taking pride in their work. They might feel it is conforming, or that this particular job is just a means to an end, a step along the way, so there is no reason to put in the energy to connect.

Without connection, without pride, work is not fun.

When you're open to connection and take pride in your work, work is fun.

You aren't compromising when you decide to take pride in your work. You are choosing to enjoy your time.

When It's Not Up to You

The people who can grasp the importance of taking pride in their work early on in their careers are special and, unfortunately, somewhat rare. Most of the time, this is because we don't feel like we are where we are supposed to be. We don't feel like our talents are fully appreciated, and we think our first few jobs are little more than stepping stones to where we really ought to be.

And there is some truth to that.

The special ones say, "So what?" Even if their parents made them take the job in high school, they find a way to fully show up.

Showing up early and often is the best way to get in the habit of taking pride in your work. You don't have to work at the same place for decades because you take pride in something, but the sooner you start taking pride in your work, the earlier you'll be on the path to making your work fun.

Here are a few questions to ask yourself if you want to jump-start the pride process at your current gig:

- Who in the company do I admire most, and why do I admire them?
- Is there a mission-based volunteer opportunity that I can participate in?
- What am I responsible for, and how can I make it better?

A quick side note: If you can't take pride in your company as a whole because of something about it that is against your morals, and you also can't afford to stop working there, try to take pride in your department. Or, in a way that doesn't negatively impact your coworkers, see if you can make positive change within the organization in a way that makes you proud.

When It's Up to You

At every step of the way, there is an easy way, and there is a right way.

The tough part of being a great leader is that the right way is going to be more difficult. Pride comes from layering decision after decision you are proud of despite the difficulty in making those decisions.

The truth is, it's tough to take pride in your work all the time. The real world is complex and difficult, and painful decisions are part of it.

Paying out a generous profit share or a bonus, when you can afford it, is something some great leaders do. Great leaders also don't pay out a profit share or bonus when the company can't afford it. It's easy to take pride in the former, but not so much the latter. Both are great, pride-worthy decisions.

If you're a decision-maker and you don't take pride in your work already, or you just want to take more pride in your work, the recipe is pretty simple: Turn up the volume on making decisions you are proud of. Get a little bit closer to failure by pushing the boundaries of what your company can do that is good.

Here are a few questions to ask yourself if you are a decision-maker who wants to take more pride in your work:

- Have we defined our company purpose? Are we living it out?
- What do I care about, and how can I inject more of that into work?
- How can I inspire others to get more involved in their work?

CHAPTER 5

Remember to Play

POP-MAKING OLYMPICS

Here's how we make our pops.

If there are any add-ins like whole pieces of fruit or cookies, they are added one by one to the pop molds first. Next, the liquid pop mix is scooped from a stainless-steel barrel and poured into the molds. A wooden stick is set into the mold, and it all gets placed in a machine for 20 minutes or so to freeze them. Then the individual ice pops are removed from the mold and finally put in a package.

Repeat. Repeat. Repeat. Repeat. Repeat.

This is the basic process for pops you make in your home freezer, and it's basically the same process Unilever, the Popsicle behemoth, uses in its factories to make upward of two hundred thousand Popsicles per factory each day.

At the industrial scale, this is all done with sophisticated equipment. A mixture goes in on one side of a football field–long machine, and boxes of frozen pops come out the other side.

At King of Pops, each of those steps is done by hand.

Handmade doesn't mean a whole lot anymore. With no legal definition, it instead is used as a marketing term to appeal to our nostalgic sensibilities.

Our stainless-steel molds make 28 pops—two rows of 14—at a time.

For each pop we make, someone places a stick into a hole a couple millimeters wider than the pop stick filling up the grid pattern. The stick slides down a tube until 80% of the stick, including the secret message on each one, is covered. There is a satisfying metallic thump each time a stick lands at the base of the stick holder.

A stick aligner is then placed over the 28 sticks and clamped shut to hold them in the place while the mixture is frozen.

Placing these sticks by hand doesn't make our pops taste any better. It's something that seems like it should be done by a machine. We own the machine that does this. Unfortunately, it is sitting in one of our warehouses, collecting dust.

Every couple of years, we set it up and commit to implementing it in our process. And without fail, it will break, and we'll revert to placing them one by one by hand. We end up spending more time working on fixing a machine to do the work for us than it would take to do the work ourselves.

As you can imagine, this monotonous task is not anyone's favorite. On a new employee's first day, after getting introduced to each of the pop-making stations, they typically end up dropping sticks for hours. There's not much to it, and it needs to get done.

Most manufacturing is some version of this. Scale is created by efficiently repeating tasks over and over. The art is designing a great process and problem-solving when things go wrong, but when things go right, it can become boring.

To offset this boredom, in our third year, we created the Frosty Freak Olympics.

We had grown to a point where our team was beginning to specialize, and the folks who spent most of their time making pops worked a standard Monday-through-Friday schedule.

After a long week, energy would be dragging by Friday afternoon. Amid this energy lull, the Frosty Freak Olympics were born.

There were no prizes, but you did get the glory that comes with your name being at the top of a list on a whiteboard.

Every task turned into an event.

We'd pour the molds without a scale and weigh after the fact to see who was able to pour with the most precision. There were team events like who could bag and seal one hundred pops the fastest.

But the event everyone really cared about was the stick sprint: who could get 10 molds—280 sticks—into the stick aligners the fastest? If a stick fell to the ground, a second was added to your time.

Lots of styles emerged.

Everyone would be timed, and the top two times were pitted against each other to determine a champion for the week.

We'd all make our way into the production room for the finals. We'd pick favorites and cheer, eventually crowning a champion.

In the background, we'd be setting the sticks into the molds to keep production moving forward. The silliness and ultracompetitiveness of the matter was hilarious. A monotonous task was transformed into play, and for an hour or two each week, we felt like children. The next week during the contest in our usual day-to-day, the best strategies were implemented, and the process started to happen faster and faster.

The Frosty Freak Olympics brought everyone together and was a perfect way to put a bow on production for the week.

Incorporating play into your work is a great way to get more eyes and hands on a project. It can help rally the troops to complete a big surge or bring in fresh eyes and perspectives to a project that is stuck.

WORK AND FUN AREN'T OPPOSITES

Work doesn't usually feel like play.

I arrive around 9 AM each day, review my calendar, and check my email.

I attend the smorgasbord of meetings on my calendar and try to complete some tasks as time allows.

If my normal schedule was audited by a third party, they would conclude that there was no play to be found.

Why is this?

As parents, we closely monitor how engaged our children are. We go out of our way to curate activities. We bring them to the playground and consciously schedule playdates.

Maria Montessori, the education pioneer whose name adorns thousands of schools, once said that "play is the work of the child." Her now-popular approach teaches kids real-life situations in a fun way, and it's proven to be an incredibly effective way to learn.

However, once we grow up, there is a self-imposed expectation that we should put our head down for eight hours and get stuff done, and if we're having fun, we must not be being productive.

Everyone has heard this phrase at one time or another: "Stop playing around and get to work."

These seven words sum up the cultural norm that work and play are meant to be separate. Most consider work a necessary evil to enable fun activities elsewhere.

We can all imagine scuba instructors, musicians, or video game designers having fun at work, but the rest of us place our work in the sad bucket of sacrifice.

While every job has parts that are not roll-on-the-floor-laughing fun, you are the biggest impediment to having fun at work. Separating fun and work is little more than a narrative that we willingly adopt.

Distaste for our day jobs starts in school and tends to increase as we get older, culminating in a "glorious" retirement, when we imagine we can finally start to have fun full time.

My mom is an avid gardener. Gardening is a physically demanding activity. It requires planning, physical labor, and ongoing maintenance. My mom has cut several vacations short because she needed to go home to water her plants.

Yet instead of agonizing over the hard work, she gleefully tells us she's going to "play in the dirt."

When you sign up for a fantasy football team, it's for fun. The ensuing activities are poring over spreadsheets of data, strategizing how you'll prioritize your draft, and checking in on the progress of your selections to optimize your team's performance each week.

These activities sound a lot like work, and you aren't paid to do it.

Because fantasy football is just for fun, we lightheartedly tease each other when someone messes up, boast about our success, and generally enjoy the process. For many, draft day becomes a celebration with all types of silly rituals that we enjoy with our friends.

An estimated 60 million people in the United States play fantasy sports, and the number continues to grow. You may not be a fan of fantasy sports, but if you spend time thinking about the things you enjoy doing the most, you'll identify elements of both work and fun.

The entrepreneurial solution to this problem is to figure out how to turn that pastime into a profession, but that suggestion requires an appetite for risk that not everyone is wired for. Regardless, all of us can figure out a way to inject lighthearted play into our work.

For many, play in general is something that is lacking in all facets of our life. Like exercising an atrophied muscle, creating opportunities for play takes conscious effort.

It's easy to feel like outside of meetings we should be solo practitioners, but play comes to us more easily when we're with others.

The same goes for movement. Physical activity stimulates the release of endorphins, which are natural mood lifters.

Another tactic to increase the likelihood of play at work is a change of scenery. When possible, this allows us to see things a little differently, and that change in perspective opens the door for more play.

While these small changes are not play themselves, they will begin to get you in the right frame of mind to incorporate more play into your work.

The most impactful way to incorporate sustained play into your work is to turn it into a game. In reality, work is little more than a game already. It just takes a little extra effort to identify what winning looks like and what rules must be followed.

To maximize the drama and intensity of the Frosty Freak Olympics, the events were short sprints. It would be inefficient overkill to run each production shift with this type of game. That said, creating a game out of our production goal, 50 thousand pops produced for a week, is setting the stage for more play.

The next step would be to share that number often and have a prize to celebrate if it is reached. For some people this is enough to encourage play, but if you want to take it to the next level, increase the silliness along the way.

For every five thousand pops produced, fill in the chart with no hands, hit a gong, or play a cheesy song with an associated dance move. Take the extra time to think of a prize that will set the mood. Lunch is great, but a themed lunch is better. How about a tropical-themed BYOHS (Bring Your Own Hawaiian Shirt) luau with leis, grass skirts, and tiki torches to be lit by the team-appointed MVPs?

Over the top? Yes. More fun than ordering pizza? Yes.

It will feel icky and uncomfortable the first few times you go above and beyond to create a fun environment, but it's all worth it when you hear the first few laughs.

The reality is that our work isn't that serious. Humanity has advanced far beyond the hunter-gatherer days, when a bad work-day meant you'd go hungry. And my guess is, a couple million years ago, as our ancestors searched for nuts and berries, there was probably more play than most of us enjoy today. Not to mention that anthropologists estimate the average week back then consisted of between 15 and 30 hours of work.

Regardless of the seriousness of the work, study after study shows that play improves results. There are studies linking play with creativity, problem-solving, job satisfaction, teamwork, and productivity.

The type of play hardly matters. Video games get a bad rap, but a 2019 study at Brigham Young found that newly formed work teams experienced a 20% increase in productivity after playing video games together for 45 minutes.

The Silicon Valley office culture, highlighted by countless Ping-Pong and foosball tables, were on to something, but remember, it's not about having the space to play, it's about making the time to play.

There are many factors that we can point to that remove the fun from work, starting with the Industrial Revolution, which brought a focus on efficiency and productivity, followed by the proliferation of corporations whose main objective is to maximize shareholder value.

It is understandable why managers do not prioritize play, but if we can be convinced that incorporating more play improves long-term results, my guess is that we'll see a lot more of it.

Play, just like any other management tool, should be incorporated into work for all the best reasons. It's good for the bottom line, and it's good for the individual.

NOBODY LIKES A GRUMPY POP SLINGER

On a busy day, a pop slinger will serve hundreds of customers.

We call them slingers because of the speed with which they are able to sell pops on a busy day. Getting pops to the people is their singular focus, and the transaction is little more than a formality. When the stars align, a slinger can serve hundreds of guests an hour.

We don't have a script for these interactions. Our customer service training manual is embarrassingly thin, but there is one rule that we are adamant about on every single transaction.

At 10 feet, we acknowledge them.

At 4 feet, say something verbally.

It is called the 10-4 rule (we borrowed it from Zingerman's).

From that point on, we let inertia do its thing. People buying pops are ready to have a good time. This is a part of their day that they do not need to take seriously, and it's fun to meet them where they are.

The very best pop slingers can weave together a line of strangers into a one-time community that will never be together again.

People on their way to buy a pop are preconditioned to have a good time. This is their moment to lower their shoulders and let their worries subside. Much different than at a grocery store checkout, when a King of Pops line gets especially long, it is amazing to see how customers begin to work together to help move things along, answering questions and providing each other with recommendations. There is an underlying self-serving purpose of getting through the line faster, but their shared enthusiasm only heightens the experience.

By the time they make it to the front, the slinger is already teed up for a five-star rating. As someone fumbles for their credit card, the slinger answers a question that isn't getting answered quite right a few people back, injects a joke, or gives a compliment. A slinger's job as conductor is to do little more than keep the train on the tracks.

I've had the distinct pleasure of being in this flow state for thousands of hours. My absolute favorite is when a customer-turned-friend sits down on the ground next to the cart as I'm slinging pops. They're enjoying their pop and helping to keep the good vibes rolling. On a number of occasions, when the line has been particularly daunting, a customer has jumped in to help—literally doing the work for the fun of it.

These hectic days are some of my best memories. I struggled to put a name to this feeling, but when Catherine Price described "True Fun" in her book *The Power of Fun*, those moments were the first thing that popped into my mind.

As opposed to "Fake Fun," like watching mindless TV, scrolling through social media, or overeating junk food, "True Fun" happens when connection, flow, and playfulness are all present.

It is the type of fun that creates memories and makes us feel alive.

Price writes, "Playfulness is the willingness to let go of our inhibitions and simply enjoy the moment. Connection is the feeling of being united with others in shared enjoyment. Flow is the state of being so absorbed in an activity that we lose track of time and space."

I love nearly everything about her book, and her research has helped me put more thoughtful words around ideas I've been feeling for quite some time, but throughout the book she casually excludes work from "True Fun."

Work, for me, is fertile ground for "True Fun."

Her first ingredient for "True Fun"—connection—can happen between coworkers quite naturally. Everyone would agree that flow, the second ingredient, is imperative for productive work, and there are endless resources to help make this so.

But then there is playfulness.

Playfulness is the one ingredient in Price's definition of "True Fun" that does not come naturally to most adults at any point in time, especially at work. That said, our work, more than anything else, is what pushes our society forward. It continues to evolve. We have been innovating what work looks like at every turn in human history. Surely, we can figure out how to add more play to our work.

As it stands, our workforce is more disengaged than ever.

Selfishly, I want work to be more fun, but it's also the best way for leaders to stand out, push back against the inertia of society, and unlock their team's full potential.

PLAN BIG FUN

When it gets cold out, King of Pops cart sales plummet.

This doesn't come as a shock.

As if not buying something wasn't enough of a signal, some people feel obliged to verbally remind us that "it's way too cold out for pops."

And then provide us with a shrewd business tip: ". . . maybe you should sell hot chocolate!"

There is nothing more demoralizing than hearing these reminders on repeat all day, while shivering and selling close to zero pops.

After that first pop season, with a lot of uncertainty about our future, Nick and I headed south for an extended vacation somewhere warm.

This tradition continued as we added employees. It was pretty easy the first few years. We were all fairly young, and we were well acquainted with cheap hotels and hostels. We'd splurge on other things, like tickets to see *lucha libre*, all the *paletas* we could find, and at least one fancy dinner at a restaurant that we hoped would inspire us.

These trips were special for several reasons, but the most value came from creating memories with our team. When spring finally came around, we had a shared set of experiences that set the stage for more fun as we reentered our busy season.

After a few years, our team had grown beyond our ability to act as a travel agent. We were beginning to age out of the hostel scene, and the trips overall were getting too expensive.

We had a friend who worked at Sixth Man, a music cruise company, and she thought she could get us the friends and family rate for one of the trips that wasn't selling too well.

So that year, we lucked into the Weezer Cruise at a super low rate.

It was so much fun. Added to that, everything was already paid for once you got on the boat. We had a handful of preplanned times when we wanted to all meet up as a group, but other than that, we all just roamed the boat, running into each other at random times doing random things.

After a few years, we outgrew our friends and family deal, but we kept the cruise tradition alive.

The focus was on creating a time to have fun together. There was no other objective. We'd buy the worst rooms on an old boat so we could afford to invite more people.

If you worked over 30 hours a week, you got an invite. By year six, we were taking over one hundred people on the annual cruise.

It was always a fun bunch. We'd be very well represented at every karaoke event, dance party, and cannonball contest. It was cheesy but so much fun.

By the time we were back in our home port, everyone on the ship knew about King of Pops.

The cruise industry does not align with our sustainability goals as a company, but we believed our improved morale was a worthy tradeoff. We were selfish in these moments, with our focus 100% on building a healthy team. And all we had to do was create an environment where play was front and center.

When the pop season kicked off the next year, there was a spillover of enthusiasm that led to a lot of great work. Nothing creates a bond like getting peed on by stingrays when you are holding them for a group photo op.

We did these cruises every year until the COVID-19 pandemic put a long pause on cruises. We haven't figured out our path back to a winter trip for several reasons. Our business has grown beyond pops, and we've figured out ways to make the seasonality of our business less dramatic.

To add to that, my life and Nick's have changed quite a bit. Marriage. Kids. Life in general gets in the way of these types of things.

That said, it is missed. It is clear we are not as connected as a group, and I think this is a huge part of it.

Setting the stage for play is imperative. You can't just expect people to all trust each other and be willing to play.

This is where big fun comes in.

There will never be the perfect time or "enough" money, but at least once a year, go out of your way to plan something spectacular, with fun as the focus.

Think of these "big fun" moments like routine maintenance for your car. Every so often you need to add a bit of fun lubricant so it doesn't seem out of place in the day-to-day.

If you feel like your workplace is a fun vacuum, go for something big to set the tone. And be prepared to be the first volunteer for any and all hijinks because your energy will set the tone.

FUN IS FREE

The most common play-avoidance technique is your budget.

All too often people get caught up in the glitz and glamor of an event that's primary purpose is to be fun. Company outings can get expensive very fast. If you can afford them then go for it, but if you can't, don't let your budget stop you from hosting some type of event.

We once hosted a DIY prom in a large room a nonprofit we work with let us use for free. We made a photo backdrop with cardboard boxes and balloons. We collected submissions for songs to be played and made a playlist that covered classics from the last 40 years. We danced, did way too many prom poses for photos, and named prom king and queen. All in all, we spent under $400, mostly on alcohol. It was a great memory created with very little money but that required a willingness to show up, participate, and put yourself out there.

It was awesome to see King of Pops employees who had avoided their high school prom make an appearance this time around.

There is not a direct correlation between the cost of an event and the amount of fun it ends up being. A fancy event reduces the awkward feeling leaders have when they propose that people willingly participate. It's easier to ask the team to meet you at the trendiest new restaurant than it is to figure out a way to lug your grill to work, find one of the tall white classic chef hats, and cook hot dogs for everyone, but in my experience, the latter leads to just as much fun.

To be clear, I do believe spending big on fun is a wise business decision, but your financial situation should not be an excuse to put it off.

PLAY TAKES WORK

At this point, you may be thinking that this all sounds fine and well, but it's not the same where you work.

Most of us are tight on time already, and spending time planning for play seems like just another thing that needs to get done. When important deadlines are looming, adding play might be seen as slacking off.

Your job might require complete concentration. Maybe you're a surgeon, a high-rise window washer, or an electrician, and one wrong move can do serious damage to yourself and others.

Or perhaps you feel like it's just not your place to do this type of thing. You might feel like you aren't senior enough to make this kind of change, or that, truthfully, you just don't like the people you work with.

You might work at a company that has a super serious, old-fashioned, or cutthroat company culture.

However, in every instance you have a larger role than you might think in creating the work world you want to be a part of.

Jason Fried is an author and cofounder of 37 Signals, a company that has been focused on culture since it started in 1999. After decades of leading the organization, he has realized that "a company's culture is a 50-day moving average of how it is, not how it thinks it is, wants to be, or was supposed to be."

People tend to think their company's culture has been decided in a room they weren't in, long before they came around, but the reality is that it's getting reset every day.

Most companies aspire to be a great place to work. No company wants to have a bad company culture, but that's what about half of them have.

The Workplace Culture Index, a survey conducted annually by LinkedIn of over one hundred thousand employees, found that over the past decade, 49.7% of people say they have a bad culture at their workplace.

King of Pops is often heralded as having a strong company culture. I tend to agree, but there have been plenty of periods when it has dipped considerably. And I would not be shocked if someone from our team responded to the "How's your company culture?" survey negatively.

By August each year, our staff is typically pretty physically worn out. We've been going hard for six months. It feels like we've been sprinting, and we should be at the end of the finish line, but the end isn't even close. To make matters worse, August always seems to include a streak of unbearable, extreme heat, where it feels like you're inside someone's mouth each time you go outside.

Energy management is a problem, and we try our best to offset the low morale with a better strategy, improved hiring, and financial incentives.

These tactical moves are super important but only one piece of the puzzle. These are the times when we need play the most. It might seem counterintuitive, but good culture is often created from a bad situation.

The problems don't go away, but doing something to feel better about them is infinitely better than pretending like they don't exist.

In the early days, when I was single and in my mid-twenties, we'd take the team out after work for drinks, bar games, and all the typical fun nightlife stuff.

Two kids and a decade later, that option is off the table. Ideally, those same connections are happening without my knowledge, but my role in creating fun is usually reserved for before 6 PM.

How to Add Play to Your Work

Instead of every four years, the Frosty Freak Olympics happened once a month on Fridays. Just enough time to gloat about your championships, but not so long that it was forgotten.

The practice of getting more play into your day-to-day work requires both spontaneous and planned activities. Some will be hits, more will be misses. The biggest thing is that you've got to try.

You'll feel like an oaf. You'll feel your age. You'll feel uncool. You'll feel cliche.

Then all of the sudden, someone will walk up to you and do the cringeworthy secret handshake you did with them the day before. You'll have a good laugh and a valuable discussion, and realize that it's all worth it.

But don't get it twisted. All those fails—when you feel like you're falling flat on your face trying to have fun at work—are just as important as the wins. Your efforts are seen, and your bravery is appreciated even if it is met with an abundance of eyerolls.

Remember that play is fun. It's something we all know how to do.

Nobody has issues with having fun; you just need to show your people the way. Your way. And while this is "hard work," your sacrifice for the good of your team will end up being fun for you too.

To add light to your coworkers' lives is super meaningful, so spend time designing play into your schedule.

The Pop-Making Olympics, Tie-Dye Tuesdays, and pop bingo are all fun for King of Pops but may not be for anyone else.

The Lego Group has created a product called Serious Play that brings their famous blocks into the boardroom to "enhance innovation and business performance."

Ben & Jerry's has built a brand around lighthearted playfulness. Their motto, "If it's not fun, why do it?" impacts all facets of the business, from flavor creation to employee get-togethers.

There isn't a one-size-fits-all playbook for this stuff. You've got to find out what is right for you and your organization.

Google "fun activities at work," and you will most surely be disappointed.

Here are a few not-that-inspiring ideas at the top of the search results list:

- Celebrate new employees.
- Organize an office sports team.
- Institute themed days.

The truth is, these ideas are all fine and actually would be fun if you did them. But you need to put your spin on any of these to amplify the fun.

- Celebrate a new employee by making a new pop flavor in their honor.
- Start a pickleball team and challenge your opponents to hold pops while you play.
- Dress up like your favorite pop flavor.

These are ideas that I think would be fun for King of Pops but, again, wouldn't be universally fun or make much sense for non-pop-making companies.

When you are ready for play, it is ready for you. Just be sure to arrive with eager, lighthearted energy. It won't be easy, and it must come from your heart.

When It's Not Up to You

As an owner and CEO, I'm trying every day to make our company more fun, but true fun for most people in the company will not come from me. While I may be responsible for creating and managing our core values, purpose, and vision, it's not realistic for me to guarantee fun for everyone.

Leaders help to create an environment ripe for fun, and if they aren't having fun, it's less likely the company will be having fun, but each coworker is going to influence the whole.

Individuals at every level are what make up a culture.

I know this because our company core values and purpose have not changed for over a decade, but our culture and how we interact with one another changes considerably each year.

During our new-employee orientation, as we go through these core values slides and talk about our culture, I like to point out that they represent the culture now. Our company employs right around one hundred people, so if we have seven people come to orientation, I'll be sure to make the point that they make up 7% of the culture.

A good leader sets the tone for the culture, but the combination of each employee's actions is what actually creates the culture. And that culture will dictate how play shows up in your work world.

It may not happen overnight, but it's important to realize your role in creating the environment you work in. If you don't want to sit around and wait for more playful fun to happen to you, here are a few things you can try to get things started:

- Plan an event. The important thing here is that you are volunteering yourself and not creating a bunch of work for people who aren't into it. Some organizations have roles for this type of thing, but most do not. More often than not, the missing ingredient for a fun time is someone to put things together.
- Coordinate breaks. Instead of taking a break by yourself, go out of your way to incorporate your coworkers; adding

a bit of play to these breaks is sure to make the rest of the day more enjoyable.

- Be active. This might sound strange, but by incorporating more movement into your day-to-day work, you will increase your chances of play. If you're on a break or between meetings, take off your headphones and walk around.

When It's Up to You

You might not have ever been the coolest person in the room, but now, as a leader in your organization, you almost certainly are not. Leaning into your uncool status is the coolest, most useful way to facilitate play.

Here are some tips if you are actively trying to increase play in your organization:

- Don't let a flop faze you. Teams play when the circumstances are right. You may have done everything you could to inject play into work, and the energy of someone on the team might have been off for reasons outside of work. If it's a small team, that will throw off everyone. Don't let a well-intentioned effort that falls flat deter you from play. Keep trying.
- When play that you didn't plan is happening, be the first to volunteer and have fun with it. Your energy will set the tone.
- If you're at a large gathering and everything is going great, leave a little bit early. Even if you are being fun and playful, your presence may inhibit some people from letting their guard down. A leader's well-timed, quick, quiet exit can allow some people to loosen up and have more fun.

CHAPTER 6

Teamwork Makes the Dream Work

OUR FIRST BONNAROO

Bonnaroo is one of the largest music festivals in the country.

It takes place in a rural part of Tennessee, about halfway between Nashville and Chattanooga. Every year, people descend from across the country to camp, party, and listen to music.

Today there are dozens of similar events that rival Bonnaroo, but when it started in 2002, it was the first of its kind in the South.

From day one it was on our radar as a dream event for King of Pops. Nick and I had attended as fans, and the idea of slinging pops to the throngs of overheated, overserved festivalgoers seemed glorious.

We weren't the only company trying to get in. It was more or less the vending Super Bowl for food trucks, carnies, and emerging food brands like ours. Our application got denied the first three times we applied. Then in 2013, we finally got accepted.

By this point we had done some large events, but Bonnaroo was on a different level. Paul McCartney, Jack Johnson, and Tom Petty headlined a lineup of over 150 bands. Most importantly, tickets sold out, and over 90 thousand people would be attending.

It was a big deal for our little brand, and we couldn't have been more hyped. The festival took place in the middle of June, so our schedule in Atlanta was full as well. Our head count in Atlanta was just over 20 at this point in time: 10 slingers, 5 frosty freaks, 2 salespeople, a bookkeeper, a GM, Nick, and me. On this particular weekend, everyone, regardless of job title, would be out on the cart slinging pops.

We ended up with a hodge-podge team of eight for the festival. We had five cart locations that were supposed to be staffed for 12 hours a day. Our goal was to sell five thousand pops. I was nervous about our ability to execute and desperate to leave a good impression with the organizers so we'd be invited back.

Armed with entry-level camping gear and rations of peanut butter and jelly, Nature Valley granola bars, Doritos, and beer, we embarked on the journey. I drove the U-Haul, packed full of pops and gear, and two cars followed.

I checked in with the organizer on Wednesday and got our wristbands, location assignments, and a general rundown of their expectations. I nodded obediently as the organizer spewed instructions, but I was so excited that I had a hard time focusing. We set up our campsite and settled in for the night.

Bonnaroo consists of a fenced-in stage area called Centeroo and 10 themed pods that act like mini town centers across the campgrounds. We were assigned two cart locations near the stages, and the other three in pods over a mile away from our campsite.

The first day of the festival, Thursday, is for hardcore fans and a warm-up for people to arrive and get familiar with the grounds, but we were eager to get started. It took us several hours to get our carts in order and push them to the far-flung locations.

We sold effectively nothing that first day. The campground locations were nearly empty, and one of the carts near the stages was positioned right next to a Ben & Jerry's truck that was giving out free ice cream.

Years later, we'd learn that festivalgoers are still satisfied with the food options they packed for themselves on day one and are consciously trying to hold on to their money. Still, the dejected, tired feeling sits with you. A combined 50 hours of vending and pushing carts across miles of gravel roads for less than 50 pops sold stings big-time, and as a result, the vibe of our group was already on the rocks.

Luckily, each day got better and better.

I'll never forget sitting on top of the box truck, listening to Paul McCartney's headlining set with a couple of slingers who had already put in 12-hour days. As we counted cash, we could see the corner of the stage and hear it perfectly. He played "Hey Jude," one of my favorites, during the encore, and as I toasted my coworkers-turned-friends, it was hard to believe this was my job. A few minutes later, a private jet the size of a commercial airliner flew directly over us—it was McCartney getting out of there. It turns out camping in the middle of Tennessee is not his jam.

The festival turned out great. But make no mistake, it was very hard work. We all walked so many miles, frantically trying to keep pops frozen in the triple-digit heat, and then stood for hours on end trying to sell them.

By the end we were completely worn down, blistered, and burned out.

As the festival ended, we all came together and positioned our carts into a circle at the main stage. We had surpassed our goal, and it was time to celebrate.

We took turns vending as Tom Petty played the last set of the festival. We traded pops for food with every vendor we could find and put together a buffet of corn dogs, grilled cheese, noodles, doughnuts, tacos, and pizza. We laughed giddily, knowing we were living a story together we wouldn't soon forget (and we'd be sleeping in regular beds soon). Somehow the exhaustion faded away, and we stayed up late partying together.

The hard work was all worth it, and we've been invited back each year since then.

More importantly, once we got home, our group of eight started working more effectively together. With a challenging shared experience under our belt, the basics back home felt more achievable than ever.

It was cool that we had to bring a team that normally focused on different facets of the business because they got a chance to sweat together on an even playing field. A young pop slinger looks at a bookkeeper differently once they realize they share a favorite band and saw them play together.

There is little debate that a strong team culture is helpful to the success of an organization. Study after study reinforces this. Not to mention the abundance of overused inspirational quotes so popular they go in one ear and out the other:

*"If you want to go fast, go alone. If
you want to go far, go together."*
—*African proverb*

*"Alone we can do so little; together
we can do so much."*
—*Helen Keller*

"Teamwork makes the dream work."
—*Unattributed, but often uttered at King of Pops*

Even better, and also unsurprising, studies show that working as a team makes work more fun.

A study published in the journal *Frontiers in Psychology* found that when people are working on a team, they are more likely to have fun and be engaged. Teamwork can also help to reduce stress and burnout.*

However, just because we all seem to want more teamwork doesn't mean we know how to create it.

There is not an agreed-upon playbook for building a great team.

A strict regimen of trust falls and another bowling outing are, like the teamwork quotes above, overdone and likely to fall flat.

During my brief stint in corporate America, I went to quite a few thoughtfully planned dinners and parties. I appreciated these efforts. I was the guy who would take a to-go plate home with

---

* Shengmin Liu et al., "The Influence of Individual and Team Mindfulness on Work Engagement," *Frontiers in Psychology* 10 (January 21, 2020), doi .org/10.3389/fpsyg.2019.02928.

me, but those "team bonding activities" never seemed to create better teams.

At the coffee station the next morning, I didn't feel more connected to my coworkers as they groggily filled their mugs next to me.

What was missing from those team bonding activities? What did our Bonnaroo adventure have that those other carefully planned corporate activities didn't?

The travel festivals continue to be an important piece of our business, but more important than the money is the lasting team camaraderie that is created. After working a festival together, coworkers overcome day-to-day challenges more smoothly for the rest of the pop season. A staffing constraint led us to a team-building strategy more impactful than any contrived team-building event with a large budget.

It was a big day when we graduated from our first pop-making machine, the one that made 88 at a time, to one that was five times that size. We picked it up in Florida, and when they loaded it onto my pickup truck with a forklift, it bottomed out my suspension.

We slowly made the trek back to our kitchen, and when we arrived, our team of 10 or so slowly trickled out to look in amazement at our new machine. This was going to be a game changer.

Slowly it dawned on us that we had no way to get the thousand-plus-pound machine out of the truck.

Little did we know another impromptu team-building opportunity was upon us. With a combination of a dozen ramps we used for loading our carts, cinder blocks, and brute strength of 10 humans, we got it into our kitchen. Luckily no fingers were lost in the process.

Those 10 people looked at that machine, and each other, differently from that point on.

Over the years, we identified four things that fast-forward the team bonding process:

- First, there needs to be a change of scenery.
- There needs to be a very clear, shared goal, and everyone needs to be in it together—all hands on deck.
- There needs to be a struggle that is physical in nature. This is the hardest part, as our natural tendency is to avoid hard physical work of any sort. And while we may get to it kicking and screaming, once we are actually doing it, especially with a team, we end up having fun.
- Once the goal is met, there has to be a celebration, no excuses.

When our heart is pumping fast and we don't have time to think through every decision, we get into our flow state quickly. Without our offices to retreat to, connection comes more naturally, and options for moments of play naturally emerge.

A shared struggle helps people assume the best in one another, because they've witnessed firsthand how hard they are willing to work for one another. There is a teamwork halo effect that spreads beyond that location and time.

It works better than the aforementioned trust falls and bowling outings because the real person emerges. In our day-to-day work, it is easy to put up a facade. We adapt to our surroundings and present what we interpret to be appropriate for the setting. When you are working close to your physical capacity as a team, there isn't enough energy to keep up the facade.

One of King of Pops' core values is "get sweaty" for this very reason. Sometimes we need a nudge to be active with each other, and these moments tend to be peak memories and a heck of a lot of fun.

These days, our headcount is 10 times the size it was for our first festival, and our schedule has stabilized. A plan is in place to regularly execute a large event like Bonnaroo, and we have a forklift in each of our warehouses.

Still, we go out of our way to schedule opportunities for the team to work together in nonroutine ways. There is no way around it: struggling together forms the team bond.

A shared experience will create a halo effect that provides some good team vibes, but without maintenance, this will wear off over time.

To keep the teamwork train on the tracks, you'll need one more thing. The more of it the better, and that thing is *hoopla*.

THE WORK VACUUM

When I worked at the newspaper, most nights ended with a completed story. The rest of the team was in a similar situation, and after rushing to get our work done by deadline, we'd pat each other on the back and celebrate together.

Every. Single. Night.

Together, we'd completed another newspaper that was ready to go out into the world.

Working at a newspaper is unique in that sense. Most work does not have that built-in daily cadence. We may create monthly quotas or quarterly budgets to artificially manufacture a timeframe to focus on, but in the back of our minds, we know nothing dramatically changes if the numbers come in a day earlier or later.

I certainly felt this contrast after leaving the newspaper and landing at AIG.

Goals were created and a due date existed, but it was all fuzzy and out of focus.

I'd be all in on a project, and once it was completed, there was little to no fanfare. In fact, the projects tended to be either disregarded or extended to include something that was not initially contemplated.

My job, more or less, was to compile and organize data. I'd combine sources that didn't talk to each other and make sure everything lined up properly. They assigned new people, like me, states with small populations. Fewer people means fewer accidents, less data to organize, and less money to lose.

I started with North Dakota, and as colleagues were laid off, I was "promoted" to work on larger states. I remember working on a report for Utah. It felt like the big time. Utah had four times as many people as North Dakota, and instead of the typical day or two, it took two weeks to get all the data put together.

Once it was complete, I proudly loaded the file onto a USB drive, because it was too large to email, and walked it over to my boss's office. He wasn't there, so I left it on his desk with a note.

I wasn't expecting a whole lot of fanfare, as it was standard stuff, but I never heard even a peep about the report.

This is pretty typical. That's what work is, right? When one project ends, another begins. There isn't a whole lot of hoopla to celebrate.

And that is a darn shame because hoopla is fun.

I should have done a little fist bump, with explosion, to myself that day. I should have done my best attempt at a moonwalk out of the room and treated myself to some of the out-of-season pumpkin spice creamer once I made it to the break room.

Instead, I was a sad puppy looking for a pat on the back that never happened.

What I didn't understand then is that that sad puppy feeling was something I could control.

HAVE MORE HOOPLA

As a leader at King of Pops, I regularly find myself falling victim to a hoopla-free work malaise.

The proliferation of work productivity tools has kept the next task always at the ready. If we're lucky, we get a celebration emoji, then we move on. This is OK for most things. We don't need a parade for sending an email, filing a paper, or answering a phone call, but our teams would be well served to celebrate more.

And from my preliminary research, more parades never hurt anyone.

My wife and I joke about the amount of affirmation a football player gets after a good play. It starts with a little dance, then some flying chest bumps with the nearest teammates, then a cute "We did that" moment with the coach, then it concludes with dozens of high fives and secret handshakes on the sideline.

Imagine if your work was like that. It would be awesome and hilarious: Bill from the receiving team was able to count all the boxes accurately, so he flings his clipboard in the air and high-steps through the warehouse, reminding everyone how great he is.

Sports are so much fun because success is so well defined. There is a beginning and an end, a winner and a loser.

We all crave a sense of accomplishment. We all want to win, and those wins feel so much sweeter when someone recognizes them. There are a few primary reasons why we so regularly skip the celebrations and go right to the next thing we are supposed to do at work.

The first is that winning is not usually a clear thing in the workplace. We haven't defined what success looks like. We haven't taken the time to break the work up into goals that can be accomplished. So we don't know if we've won or not.

If your only goal is to have $10,000,000 in sales for the year, you only have one opportunity to celebrate at the end of the year.

If you break it up into weekly chunks, things get more interesting.

You need to have $192,308 in sales each week to be on track. But don't stop there.

This might be a good goal for the sales team, but a lot of things need to happen before that goal is even possible.

Within that number there are goals for different teams.

If you're an ice pop company, that means you have a goal for how many pops need to be produced each week to support that goal. Manufacturing is often a thankless job. It is expected to happen with little fanfare, but imagine how meaningful it would be if the sales team came by to congratulate them after a "normal" week when things were on track.

You need people to deliver all these pops to the right ware-houses, then eventually to customers. Again, the expectation is that this happens on time and with a smile. How could that piece of the puzzle be broken down into an easily definable goal?

For every business there are a lot of "normal" things that need to happen in order to achieve the sales number.

Spending some time defining goals for each of these is an invaluable task. More opportunity for wins leads to more celebra-tions, and more momentum for your team.

Step one is hard. Step two is harder.

We need to give credit generously.

When it is a clear victory, there is a tendency for a manager to temper excitement. For whatever reason, in manager land, our brains regularly jump to the conclusion that the circumstances changed to make the success a given. And the feeling is that the success wasn't earned, it was gifted, thus hoopla is not necessary or appropriate.

Back to our football example: if the quarterback makes a mis-take, drops the ball, and someone on his team picks it up in the end zone, the player who scores is still pretty darn proud of them-selves. The crowd goes wild, celebrations ensue, and the hype level is pretty indecipherable from a "legitimate" great play.

We often do the opposite in the work setting. It is common to blame the failure on the individual and credit success to the circumstances.

Here is what I mean in King of Pops terms.

Let's say we have a successful event and sell completely out of pops. My first thought is, "That was a great event. We could have done better . . . We should have brought more pops!"

If there's bad weather and slingers don't sell very many pops, my first thought is, "They are making excuses." I think through opportunities missed—they should have been more engaged with the customers, invited them to stay dry under their rainbow umbrella, or found a better location. I might think, "*Where is the team spirit? Don't they care about our quarterly goals?!*"

You could just think that I'm a jerk, but before we go there, run the circumstances through your head. If everything lines up perfectly for someone on your team, do you celebrate them?

The truth is the weather plays an important factor in our success at an event. We sell exponentially more pops if it's sunny and 90°F versus rainy and 50°F, but it isn't "fair" to attribute the win to the circumstances and the failure to the team.

We know in the back of our mind that our results are always a combination of the circumstances and the effort put forth, but if we get caught up in figuring out if an effort was good or bad considering the circumstances, we risk celebrating nothing.

To avoid this, we need to celebrate far more wins far more often. The more wins we recognize, the more opportunities for hoopla.

In sports, broadcasters excessively use the word *momentum* in their analysis. The best coaches know the right buttons to press at the right time to get results. In work, we don't think so much about momentum, but managers should be using the same tactics that coaches use.

When we are confident, having fun, and celebrating our wins with more and more elaborate hoopla, everything seems to fall in place. A bit of good news allows us to relax and better execute our plan. We are excited for the next step and get a lot more done.

Chances are, most work goals need to be more well defined. Once you find that clarity, dust it off, break it up into smaller pieces, and shine a light on the wins along the way to bigger goals.

A good goal should be a challenge. If you're achieving your goal every single time, you aren't pushing yourself hard enough. So if you miss it, pick yourself up and move on.

But if you hit your goal, please, please, please celebrate. Do a dance, ring a bell, eat a churro. Do something fun and talk to someone about it.

YOU ARE 100% RESPONSIBLE

If you close your eyes and try to picture a great teammate, what comes to mind?

For me, it is someone optimistic, fun, and collaborative. It's someone who makes everyone around them better.

We all strive to be this person, and it seems fair that if we do our part, our teammates should as well. Like most relationships, a 50-50 arrangement seems to fit. We are only partially responsible for the success of the team.

My mind was blown when I attended my first ZingTrain training. The first thing I learned, and subsequently signed, was their training compact. The document laid out expectations for me and for the trainers. That simple idea of putting our commitment in writing was powerful.

However, the mind-blowing part for me was on the next page, which explained that a successful training would not be achieved with a 50-50 relationship. Instead, we would both be 100% responsible for the training's success.

"While the trainer's role is to document clear expectations, provide the training resources, and recognize and reward performance, the trainee is ultimately responsible for the effectiveness of his/her training," said Maggie Bayless, ZingTrain's founding partner. "You can require someone to attend a class or a training shift, but you can't make them learn. We're each responsible for learning what we need to know to do our jobs well."

The same concept can be applied to management and goal setting.

The manager's goal is to document clear expectations, provide guidance, and recognize and reward performance. Both the manager and each member of the team are ultimately responsible for their success.

And if I were to add one thing, it would be that it is also 100% up to everyone to celebrate those wins.

You don't need to wait for anyone else. Walk into your next meeting, and go around the table high-fiving everyone for meeting a goal that week that typically gets ignored. I bet that meeting will be more fun and effective than normal.

There is nothing to lose, and everything to gain.

MY BRO, OFFICE BESTIES, AND WORK WIVES

For most of my life, I've been taught to use the words *us* and *we* when referring to anything positive, and *I* and *me* when referring to anything negative. It's a practice that has been hammered into my head by coaches, teachers, and my parents.

More often than not, you aren't fully responsible for your success, and avoiding *I* and *me* encourages you to lean into the idea of teamwork. Not to mention, it makes you sound a little less into yourself.

There is an added side benefit when your company is super small, in that it makes it sound more substantial than it really is.

There is one King of Pops decision, however, that I have to take full credit for. I was the only paid employee in the company, so my friends and family would have been worried about me if I told them that *we* had just made a big decision, because it was a decision I had to make 100% on my own.

It just so happened to be the best business decision I've ever made.

By the middle of May that first year, it was clear that King of Pops was going to make it. It was unclear if "making it" meant a few thousand dollars in profit or the lifelong pursuit of the perfect pop, but things were quickly escalating beyond something I could handle on my own.

Six weeks after the first pop was sold, my brother Nick and I were at Restaurant Depot buying supplies.

At that time Nick was a prosecutor. He had finished law school a couple years prior and spent Monday through Friday in the courtroom, arguing cases. I was crashing on his couch, and he was helping out at King of Pops on nights and weekends.

As we walked the aisles gathering supplies, I asked him if he wanted to quit his lucrative law gig and join King of Pops full time.

He knew I needed the help, and I wanted a true partner.

I offered to make him a 50-50 owner in the business if he would come on full time. If he couldn't, I was going to have to hire someone else just to keep up.

As we browsed blenders and mop buckets, I remember forecasting together how many pops we'd need to sell in order for this to be a good decision.

We made a nice profit for every pop we sold, but we were selling them for $2.50 each, so we'd have to sell quite a few to match his salary as a lawyer.

Without pen or paper, we calculated how many pops we'd have to sell that year to support two people. I remember landing on the number one hundred thousand.

It's hilarious to me that major milestones always land on nice round numbers. One hundred thousand pops didn't feel entirely impossible, but it was definitely a stretch. At that point, we were making 88 pops at a time. Each batch took two or three hours, so if everything went perfectly, it would be more than a full-time job for each of us just to make the pops, let alone sell them.

Somehow we had faith that we would figure it out. Before we checked out from the store, we had agreed to become business partners.

In that moment nothing had actually changed, but there was a huge weight lifted from my shoulders.

Over the years we've accomplished all kinds of things that once seemed impossible. Somehow, when two people agree to an audacious goal, it seems more believable and thus more doable. When they care about each other, that lift is amplified because they don't want to let each other down.

We didn't know it at the time, but Nick and I complement each other very well.

The idea of "fake it 'til you make it" implies that there are some people out there who aren't faking it. In a way, we've made it, but even now, 15 years later, it feels like we've got a lot to learn. That learning process just happens to be much more pleasant with a partner.

There is a saying: "It's lonely at the top." Well, it doesn't have to be.

It is only lonely if you keep something to yourself. But if you decide to solve problems together, it isn't lonely. Nick and I talk about top-of-mind things, big-picture things, and personal life things every week.

Sometimes it is a scheduled meeting, like our Friday "Bros Pump & Pow-Wow," where we lift weights while chatting, then dive into an agenda over coffee afterward. But most of the conversation happens ad hoc. A phone call while he's driving home from a work trip in Charlotte can go on for hours after my family has gone to sleep, as we are both super invested in the results.

During COVID-19, every week, Nick was driving the transfer truck between cities to redistribute the inventory for our distribution company P10. We got on the same page about nearly every work topic as he drove from Atlanta to Nashville to Charlotte to Charleston then back to Atlanta.

I rode shotgun with him on one of these trips, and I think it may have been one of the best meetings we've ever had. In addition to making plans and getting onto the same page, I was introduced to truck-stop culture and the advantages of Pilot versus Love's, and felt like a giddy four-year-old each time we pulled through the weigh stations.

Plenty of advisers cringe when I tell them my brother and I own the business 50-50. "How will you make tough decisions if your votes count equally?!"

For Nick and me, that hasn't been a problem. We just talk things through.

The real benefit, however, isn't tactical. The continuous conversation makes the work so much more fun. As things come up, we are constantly brainstorming and discussing new ideas. Our conversations have so much backstory and context that it is unlike anything else I have in my life.

My relationship with Nick is special but not entirely unique. I regularly catch my wife still in her car in the garage talking to her best work friend long after she's gotten home—not quite ready to hang up and officially wrap up her day. I do my best to stay up to speed and love talking to her about what she has going on, but I simply cannot grasp the nuances in the same way as someone who is going through it with her in real time every day.

She's a scientist at the CDC, so her work could not be more different from mine, but the kind of relationship she has with her best work friend could be cultivated in any field. Having someone that you trust and confide in at work amplifies your work experience and makes it more enjoyable at every level and in every industry.

I observe this across our company. When someone has a close relationship with a coworker, regardless of their department or stature, they just seem happier. They stick around longer and are more productive.

It makes sense, and study after study backs this up. The data show that having a close relationship with someone at work makes you more effective and more likely to report a positive work experience.

We've tried as a company, without much success, to pair people up and encourage these relationships, but the truth is they need to happen authentically on their own. It is unlikely that your manager or your direct report will fill the role of office bestie, but beyond that they can be found anywhere.

Take the time to seek out and cultivate these special relationships, and your work will become more fun.

HOW TO BUILD GREAT TEAMS

Teamwork is the not-so-secret sauce of great organizations. It is worth investing in and cultivating, but the path to building a team is nonlinear.

There isn't a single thing to focus on.

I remember being frustrated when I was single. A common bit of advice that I couldn't fully appreciate at the time was "You'll find someone when you stop looking."

Searching for teamwork is similar. It comes not from desperation but from constantly showing up for the people around you.

A strong team will naturally emerge if the ideas from the previous chapters are alive and well:

- If there is a story that provides meaning and that people can get behind.
- If everyone is not in a rush to get to the next thing.
- If there is a shared sense of ownership.

- If there is a sense of pride.
- If there is time for play.

Most people inherently understand and agree that teams are more effective than individual contributors working alone. But we do not always appreciate that they are more fun.

A great team will amplify the positive characteristics of work.

When It's Not Up to You

Teams are the most fun when everyone is pulling their weight and has a clear role. While some may get more attention and accolades, each person is essential. Understanding and embracing your current role is a great way to be a good teammate.

Being on a strong team is helpful for your growth as you have a chance to observe other roles you are interested in. Your teammates will share with you what they've learned, and you will return the favor to those who are interested in learning more about what you are doing.

Start here when you're ready to get more deliberate about becoming a good teammate:

- Make an effort to get to know people on your team beyond the surface level. Checking in with your team is not a top-down responsibility. Be sure you're doing your part.
- Seek out ways to help others succeed beyond your accountabilities.
- Do the little things. Whether it is a favor outside of work or a high five when you walk by, these little moments add up.

When It's Up to You

Surprise! It's not ever really up to you. At least not fully.

You can't "will" a great team to happen on your own; it requires a group effort.

However, you are the captain of the team. You're responsible for setting the tone and setting others up for success.

It's not fair to hope for a great team if you're unwilling to do all the things it takes to be a good teammate as well. Make sure you're doing everything on the list in the previous section.

Here are a few additional things to consider when assembling your team:

- Define the team. Having a handful of people who are kind of in and kind of out dilutes and confuses the whole team mentality. There is no limit to how many teams you can be on, but it isn't helpful if everyone is on all the teams.

- Create opportunities for the team to work together live. It's still ideal for this to happen in real life, but if you manage a remote team, planning times when everyone is working on the same issue at the same time virtually is a close second.

CHAPTER 7

Work Within the Tension

WORK FEELS LIKE WORK MOST DAYS

The process of making an ice pop is very simple.

So simple in fact that the Popsicle in our country was invented by accident.

The story goes that 11-year-old Frank Epperson had mixed a powder with water to make a soda. He got distracted and left the mixture and a wooden mixing spoon outside overnight. When he woke up the next morning, the soda had frozen.

The boy pulled out the frozen concoction using the stick, and it tasted delicious. Frank would go on to make these new concoctions for his friends and family, until he decided to get a patent for the idea 18 years later, in 1923.

He sold the rights to a dessert company, the John Lowe Company, which is responsible for popularizing the Popsicle brand.

Popsicles took off, so much so that one hundred years later, the word *Popsicle* is used by many, myself included, as a generic term for a frozen treat on a stick.

When I started King of Pops, we had the tagline "Handcrafted Popsicles" below our logo to help describe our offering.

This innocent description would come back to haunt me.

It was a beautiful day in May 2011, my second season doing the King of Pops thing. I had just unloaded my cart, set up my umbrella, and written the flavors on my chalkboard when a nice lady approached and purchased a dozen pops. At that time, selling a couple hundred pops was a good day, so notching a dozen sales in the first few minutes was a great feeling.

We exchanged a few pleasantries, and I waited for her to scurry back to her car to find a freezer for her purchase.

But she didn't.

Instead, she handed me a document that oozed the look of an official matter. This was the type of document that I intended to stay away from in my new line of work. The thick paper stock seemed to add to the seriousness of the matter.

Her disposition didn't match that of the document. She wasn't smiling but seemed to be enjoying herself. Before I could read it, she explained to me that the word *Popsicle* was a trademarked term, and I could not use it in my product description.

She went on to walk me through the history of the product's success, which led to the brand name becoming a generic term. Escalator, Yo-Yo, Thermos, and Zipper are a few examples of brands that over time were unable to protect their trademark because of their success.

To avoid that fate, Unilever, the now owners of the word *Popsicle*, have to send lawyers like her around to deliver the fancy paper and bad news to people that typically don't know better.

As the lady returned to her car, my mood plummeted.

Between customers for the rest of the day, I struggled to come up with words to describe what we were selling. I worried that the word *pop* alone might be confused with sugary, carbonated drinks. If we called it an "ice pop," it would not properly represent the rich, creamy flavors like Chocolate Sea Salt or Banana Puddin' that were among our bestsellers.

A month or so passed, and the lawyer came back again. My blood pressure shot up as she approached. I felt my world crashing down and was waiting for a pair of agents in nondescript black outfits to put me in handcuffs and take me to jail for using the word *Popsicle*. Instead, she asked how I was doing, bought a dozen more pops, and handed me the paper again.

That season she came back a handful of times. She'd buy more pops and drop off another cease and desist letter. She was clear and consistent each time but so darn nice about it.

Basically, if we didn't stop using the word *Popsicle*, they would make the case in court that they lost sales because of product confusion. Meaning the customer thought they were buying a product they weren't.

We felt strongly that that would not be the case, and my brother and I brazenly considered standing up to the billion-dollar brand.

At this moment it felt like everything was on the line. The situation was frustrating and terrifying, and certainly not fun. I would work myself up into a mini rage every time the thought of removing the word *Popsicle* from our branding crossed my mind.

Meetings on the topic weren't any better. In the back of our heads, Nick and I knew we had the same goal, but as we aligned and started to defend certain ideas, we started to get frustrated with each other.

It was a terrible feeling. A weight that we could not lift.

The worry overshadowed all the good that was happening around us. Bad news has a way of doing that. Like a batch of pops with two pounds of salt added instead of two ounces, everything felt like a waste.

In the end, our good judgment got the best of us. Slowly over the next year, we removed the word from our branding, and eventually, the lady stopped bringing the fancy paper by.

In the end, nobody missed the word *Popsicle* in our branding.

POPS AND A PANDEMIC

Almost a decade later, something far more dramatic came to try and shut down our business.

By 2019, our business had grown to just under $10 million in sales. Our midsummer payroll ballooned to over three hundred employees, and we sent out hundreds of carts every week to sling pops at the largest events across the South.

We were profitable and growing each year.

By March 2020, all those things we'd worked so hard for were in doubt. Everything we thought we knew about running our business was about to change.

COVID-19 was here, and it was so much bigger than any of our plans.

Looking back on the first half of 2020, there wasn't a single moment when things came into focus that we wouldn't be having a normal year. It was a never-ending crescendo of unbelievably bad news. Bad for humanity and seemingly particularly bad for our type of business.

We were wrapping up our annual company symposium in February when news of the first cases emerged. This symposium was the largest and most expensive meeting in our company history. We had flown in trainers from Michigan, put up the out-of-towners in nice Airbnbs, and scheduled fun activities for the evenings. It was one of those moments when I had to pinch myself because our business seemed so legit.

When the first cases were reported in Washington, it became clear this might have an impact on us as well. My first thoughts at the time were disappointment that the momentum from this awesome meeting was going to be dampened.

If only that was the extent of it.

From there, the news got worse.

Case counts soared, gatherings started to get canceled, and eventually lockdowns were put in place.

I'll never forget when I heard the news that MLB had postponed opening day. Baseball season and ice pop season align, April through October, and the idea of something with so much history and money pushing pause put things into perspective for me.

As days of the unknown turned into weeks of fearing the worst, we knew we had to make some big changes. In less than a month, hundreds of events King of Pops was supposed to attend were canceled, and it was unclear how we would stay open.

However, a strange thing happened. As we barreled toward financial ruin, a sense of togetherness emerged.

The feeling that our circumstances were not 100% in our control turned into a superpower. Instead of the "more work" feeling when a new idea was presented, it was met with enthusiasm. When a counterpoint was brought up, it wasn't met with resistance. Instead, it was truly considered.

The first pandemic in over one hundred years put our paltry pop issues in perspective. The government deemed us "essential," and we were able to operate during the lockdowns, but seeing so much struggle in the world highlighted the trivial nature of our work.

The virus and the unknowns of the pandemic were much scarier than missing a rent payment or not meeting a quota.

We jumped into action and diverted as much of our staff as possible to support our wholesale opportunities. While events were no longer a thing, grocery store shelves were empty, and distributors were struggling to keep up.

In two weeks, we created a new online store to deliver our products and dozens of other brands' products straight to our neighbors who had to stay home. We developed new online offerings based on the ingredients we could find in stores, ranging from vegan chili to DIY pop-tail kits that people could use to make their own ice pop–garnished cocktails at home.

While our normal King of Pops events were getting canceled, small grassroots meetups were emerging in neighborhoods and subdivisions. The disorganized nature of these gatherings made it tough for us to find them, but members of those communities started to call to see if they could borrow a cart and sling pops.

Many of them had lost their jobs and were looking to find a new source of income.

By June of that year, we had put together a reseller program that would eventually develop into our Cartrepreneur franchise opportunity. At the time of this writing, we've sold over 60 territories, and the Cartrepreneur program is responsible for selling more pops per year than our prepandemic team ever did.

Much like getting laid off from AIG or selling from carts because opening a store was going to be too expensive, COVID-19 had a handful of positive business outputs.

The silver lining of a bad situation once again led us to a business opportunity that we wouldn't have landed on otherwise.

Things, as they often seem to do, worked out in the end.

IT'S ONLY ICE POPS

As we did our best to stay in business during the pandemic, I was reminded once again that the stress and tension we normally apply to our work does not actually serve us.

We all tend to take ourselves too seriously.

I lead an ice pop company, for goodness' sake. It couldn't be less serious.

Still, if you catch me on a bad day, and you somehow missed the rainbow-painted walls and "pop" art throughout our office, you'd think I was working on something with worldly consequences. Even as I write this book about the value of work being fun, I catch myself stuck in feelings of self-appointed stress several times per week.

It's not a show; it's how I feel.

When we take pride in our work, it is natural to feel big emotions, especially when things don't go as planned. Being aware of how these emotions serve us is critical for facilitating fun at work.

The reality is that in order for our work to be fun, it has to have a purpose we are invested in. But remember, that doesn't mean we need to be uptight and serious.

There is a balance that we should seek in our work. We have to constantly remind ourselves that the weight of our work's consequences isn't world-shattering.

"It's only ice pops" has turned into a bit of a mantra at King of Pops.

When a shipment of fruit doesn't arrive on time . . . "it's only ice pops."

When we get a flat tire on our way to an event . . . "it's only ice pops."

When it rains on our busiest day of the year . . . "it's only ice pops."

In my line of work, when it may seem like the world is crashing down around us, the reality is that the worst-case scenario is that someone doesn't get a pop.

Not getting a pop is certainly a bummer, but on the cosmic scale of bummers, it's a small one.

When we think about it, most of our work stressors are not that consequential.

Coming to terms with the worst thing that could happen unlocks something within us, allowing us to loosen up and have more fun.

Think of the lawyer's lighthearted approach when delivering the cease and desist to us. She could have confronted me aggressively, threatening to shut us down if we didn't do what she wanted right away. Instead, she chose to deliver the news directly to us in a supportive, helpful way. This didn't impact the results of her work. In fact, it probably helped. What's more, I'm guessing she had fun doing it and was able to expense a whole bunch of pops.

Somewhere along the way, we internalize that work is supposed to be serious. For a few of us, that might be the case, but for many of us, it probably isn't.

If you can replace that feeling of seriousness with fun, your results and blood pressure will both improve.

THE ENDLESS PURSUIT OF PASSION

It is natural to want the tension to go away.

We perpetually feel like we are a few good breaks away from a world where we gracefully glide through our days, solving big issues and working to, as Steve Jobs famously said, "put a dent in the universe."

That is my goal too.

I've convinced myself that this is possible through King of Pops. Our company purpose is to create unexpected moments of happiness (UMOHs). The person or place doesn't matter so much as shining a light on someone and appreciating them.

People often get hung up on choosing the perfect purpose. The truth is, nearly every purpose is some version of "make the world a better place." Sometimes we overthink it, stall, and, as a result, don't identify a purpose at all.

It took us quite a while to land on ours at King of Pops, but since we did, it has become more impactful for our business and more important to me each and every year.

We say we do this for the people who receive the pops, but when we give a pop to a group that we want to recognize, it feels good internally as well.

I believe these small acts of kindness are worthwhile on their own, but more importantly, they create momentum far beyond King of Pops. I think this type of kindness can change the world.

This is what I believe on my best day. On my worst day, our purpose seems trivial and a waste of time and money. In these moments, UMOHs feel like little more than a sad marketing ploy. A nuisance on our income statement that we cannot escape.

It is important to realize that as hard as we try, we will never achieve mastery of our mood. The best we can hope for is to be aware of our less useful feelings, and try to cultivate feelings that move things forward.

It's eye-opening to think about how long humanity has been fretting about the same issues. The Stoics were wrestling with the same thoughts thousands of years ago. The ideas they came up with seem just as poignant today.

Philosopher after philosopher in ancient Greece and Rome wrote about the reality of our impermanence, the insignificance of our lives, and the importance of being useful.

The ideas bear repeating. They speak to our natural intuition to see ourselves as the center of the universe.

The Stoics' thoughts are not the types of messages embroidered on pillows at the retirement home. They are dense thoughts that remind us of how small we are.

If you aren't already familiar, here are a few quotes from the most famous Stoics to give you a taste.

Marcus Aurelius: "If you are distressed by anything external, the pain is not due to the thing itself, but to your estimate of it; and this you have the power to revoke at any moment."

Epictetus: "Life is very short and anxious for those who forget the past, neglect the present, and fear the future."

And the one I try to remind myself the most:

Seneca: "It is not the man who has too little, but the man who craves more, that is poor."

Although it is in fashion for entrepreneurs to identify with Stoic ideals, the Stoics themselves weren't particularly focused on work. However, a couple thousand miles away in Japan, a concept called *Ikigai* was emerging.

The word translates to "reason for being," but it is commonly described as the intersection of what you are good at, what you can be paid for, what you love, and what the world needs.

Over time we figure out what we're good at and what we can be paid for.

You probably have a guess, but the world has a way of letting you know if you're on the right track. One of the ways is through compensation, but most people don't have a hard time recognizing what they're good at.

When it comes to work, I don't think you ever really know what you love or what the world needs, though. You just keep guessing. You don't have to settle, but realize you may never know what you love to do.

I love my work. I know that I do, but I have yet to identify what I love about it. When I isolate an aspect of my everyday—for example, forecasting, doing quarterly reviews, or leading a meeting—it alone does not feel like something I love or that I'd want to spend my life doing.

However, somehow the combination of all those things, building something with my brother and coworkers, is all I want to do. And on my best days, I can convince myself that kindness is exactly what the world needs and what we can offer.

LET THE BAD NEWS ROLL

Picture this: I have just gotten off the phone with my brother. Somehow, 7 of our 10 freezer trucks have stopped working at the same time. One of our production lines is down, so the Frosty Freaks are working overtime to make fewer pops. A manager shoots me a text that the freezer tech isn't going to be able to make it by today, so our display freezer at our flagship King of Pops Bar will be empty for another weekend.

Just then our HR manager pops her head into my office to ask if I have a moment—never a good sign. I try my best to fake an enthusiastic demeanor and ask if everything is OK.

She looks away as she mutters the words.

"I think we have a morale problem."

This isn't how this is supposed to be, I think. *This isn't why I left corporate America.* I'm exhausted.

As she carefully weighs her words, I can tell my HR manager doesn't want to hurt my feelings. However, I know the truth she is speaking quite well.

By August each year, our freezer equipment has been pushed to its limit. Summer in the South is no joke, and there are not enough freezer techs to keep things running smoothly.

In much the same way, our staff has been pushed to the limit. Too many long shifts, too much humidity and heat, and they need a break.

Unlike freezers, humans have emotions, and in addition to the physical wear and tear, they know the hard work is not going away anytime soon. We spent all winter preparing for this, and if we don't sell as many pops as we can while the summer heat is around, we'll be kicking ourselves come January when we are short on funds.

I look back at my HR manager, unsure what to say. I've been here before. I've been here at a table like this every August, talking to various leaders about the frustrated energy in the company, for over a decade.

As much as it pains me to say it, every year there is a period when the fun vanishes. It never gets any easier.

I guess it's good that we're having the conversation, but I've resigned to the fact that we can't completely remove the feeling of tension.

We agree to address it head on in the next all-hands meeting, and I begin to write yet another companywide note addressing the issue and thanking everyone for their continued efforts. It's not much, but it is something.

Invariably, August does eventually end. In September, we get our first cool morning of the year, and this fake fall reminds us that our sprint will soon come to a close.

As much as we want only the good things in life, this simply is not an option.

With good comes bad.

Our mood is regulated by hormones and neurotransmitters that we only kind of understand. Dopamine, serotonin, and cortisol are among the most prominent, but the list goes on. They combine to motivate us one way or another.

If we flood our brains with feel-good drugs, we build up a tolerance. The good doesn't feel as good anymore, and the negative emotions are just around the corner.

I'm sure it's not really this simple, but my take is that everything is in balance, and we have to wade through the bad in order to get to the good. It's a cycle that you can either unsuccessfully resist or acknowledge and find peace in.

In this way you get to decide if you are a glass-half-empty or glass-half-full type of person. I believe more good comes to the optimists, and it is far too common for someone's first reaction to come from a place of negativity. Why not shift that? In what way is it serving you to react negatively? Reacting positively will help to rally the team, make for a better story to tell, and once again lead to more fun.

BETTER PROBLEMS STILL STING

Let's just say time travel is real, and you take a time machine back one hundred thousand years.

It's hard to imagine that you'd get many sympathy points as you tried to outline your work woes to a Neanderthal.

Imagine it's midsummer and you are accompanying a caveman to the closest berry patch to gather food for your colleagues and family. As you try to outline your present-day frustrations you are having with freezer techs and energy management, it becomes clear that your issues don't matter all that much.

After a couple hours of flies biting your exposed skin, while you worry that a predator could emerge at any moment, the insignificance of flavored ice on a stick is once again on full display.

The realization this time travel thought exercise yields isn't so different from that of a successful entrepreneur who exits a company for a life-changing amount of money and is faced with a new set of problems that most people would willingly accept without batting an eye.

What am I going to do with all this money?

What am I going to do with my time now that I don't need to work?

What is my purpose now that work is optional?

Unfortunately, time travel and life-changing sums of money are not the reality for most of us, but no matter where we are in life, we are living some version of having more opportunities and resources than we truly need. We've all gotten used to having air conditioning, unlimited entertainment on screens of various sizes, and more than enough food.

This sounds like the setup to a bad joke, but if a Neanderthal, Stoic, *Ikigai* practitioner, and former entrepreneur who just had a successful exit walk into a bar, they'd all be able to relate to the challenge of finding purpose.

They'd also each be feeling discomfort with their pursuit.

Tension is an unintended consequence of seeking purpose in your work.

The day-to-day tension will never go away. In fact, the tension is often an indicator that you are doing something that matters to you.

If you are able to find peace with this balance, you've got something more valuable than the mega yachts or the biggest berry patch in the world.

How to Work Within the Tension

Opting out of work stress requires little more than a mindset shift. It takes practice, and even then, we will all have off days. The goal is to find balance between the motivation our passion provides and the reality that we can only influence so much.

If you can put in your best effort and then accept the outcomes without all the worrying and fretting, you'll save yourself a lot of grief. Again, the goal here isn't perfection. You will not enjoy every moment of every day, but you can become aware of how you are contributing to the unpleasant feelings you are experiencing.

When you are aware that you're participating in creating your narrative of stress at work, a.k.a. making a mountain out of a molehill in the galactical grand scheme of things, that stress will become less common.

Awareness can help to get the stress to go away. An active lifestyle will help to keep it away.

Bestselling author and life coach Tony Robbins proudly takes a cold plunge in a 57-degree tub every morning. It's a habit for him now, but he does the plunges, along with a list of other common and not-so-common routines, to take care of his body. He points out that people always want to start with strategy, but they first should work on their state.

"In a different state, we're different people," he says. "Really learning to train yourself to be in an ideal state, where the best of you comes out for your family, your mission, for your world, for your coworkers. To me that is one of the most important life decisions to make."

It's hard to believe that simple things to change your state of being, like getting enough sleep, eating well, breathing, and even maintaining good posture, are going to make a big difference on your hardest workdays, but they do.

Taking care of yourself will reduce work tension and make it more fun.

When It's Not Up to You

Did you do the best you could do today? If you can answer "yes" to that question, then there is nothing more to worry about. You've done your part and are done until you go out and do your best again tomorrow.

This idea holds true throughout your career. If you are putting forth your best effort, you've earned a pass to opt out of any internal dialogue about work stress.

If you're still feeling stressed out, start here:

- Try to identify what is stressing you out. If it's more than one thing, write everything down and prioritize that list. If you're not sure where to start on your list, get help from your manager.

- If you've been assigned more than you can get done by putting forth your best effort, let your team know. Communication is key. You aren't making excuses; you're reporting on reality. Align with your manager on priorities and tell them that you'll keep them up to speed if you finish quicker than you planned.

- All work exists on a spectrum of fun and not-so-fun things to do. That is OK. Remember that your present isn't your forever. Identify parts of your current position that you'll miss as you advance in your career, and enjoy them now (or try to carry them with you to your next role).

When It's Up to You

When a decision is stressful, it means there is not a perfect answer. It might impact someone negatively or create additional headaches down the line. That's a bummer, but the stress does not change anything. Once you've done your due diligence, let it rip, and move on.

Tension is amplified when decisions to move the organization forward are postponed. Every decision you make will have an impact. At the same time, you'll never have the satisfaction of knowing if you made the right call.

When work tension is too high too often, start here:

- Ask yourself if you are postponing a decision. Just as collaborators on your team can let go of their worries if they gave it their all, you should accept the fate of your decision if you did your due diligence. The anxiety around big decisions isn't serving you. A bias to action will.

- Go for a walk. Sometimes your best effort is actually no effort at all. At a certain point, in the most stressful situations, our time and attention are not moving things forward. When this is the case, you need to reset. This could be achieved by getting outside for some fresh air, or it might require a vacation. Realize that working harder doesn't always mean better results.

- Establish your work routine. In the "always on" work world we now operate in, routine is more important and self-directed than ever. Find one that is sustainable for you over the long run and communicate your intentions with the people in your life. There will be times when you have to break from routine, but if it's happening regularly, reassess your commitments.

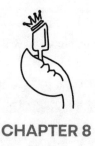

CHAPTER 8

You're Probably Thinking This Will Never Work

I've written this book from my very privileged perspective.

I was lucky to be born in the United States to two loving parents.

As a white guy who grew up in the suburbs of Atlanta, it is important to acknowledge that my experience is not universal. The worst parts of the world are things I've only watched on TV, studied in textbooks, and looked away from more than I'm proud of.

I've had bad days, but my struggles do not compare with the obstacles so many people have to face. There is so much suffering and hate in our world, and I've had the good fortune to watch most of it from afar.

Because I have not walked in those shoes, I can't say that the words in this book are applicable to every set of circumstances.

That said, I know far too many people who have won the birth lottery like me and remain miserable at work.

For most people in this situation, work is a requirement: we need to do it to earn money, but we have a support system. We have multiple safety nets.

If shit hits the fan, I know I can collect unemployment and retreat to a family member's house. At the end of the day, my family's basic needs will be met.

Still, the plan for so many is to go out and work. And while the weight of those expectations is mostly of our own making, it still feels very heavy.

We've been given this amazing gift, but we don't know what to do with it.

The options of what to work on are limitless. Among those options are earning huge sums of money and earning just enough to scrape by.

There are options that are mostly selfless humanitarian pursuits, and others that are designed to maximize prestige and power. And like most things in life, there is everything in between.

Privileged people like me are often quick to gloss over the fact that we have a choice when it comes to our work. There are far too many people without this agency, people for whom the line between survival and death is razor thin, and a missed paycheck means a missed meal for their family or a night on the street.

According to the United Nations Food and Agriculture Organization, the world produces enough food to feed everyone. It is the distribution of food that is uneven, leading to hunger in some areas and waste in others.

The same can be said for all our basic needs. Shelter, water, and clothes are all things that humanity has the capacity to provide to everyone. However, we consistently fail to distribute these things. As a result, millions of pounds of food go to waste as people starve.

The US Department of Housing and Urban Development reports that there are millions of vacant houses, yet there were 580 thousand people experiencing homelessness on a single night in 2020.* And this is in the wealthiest country on the planet.

Politics aside, society has the ability to provide what is needed.

These ideas do not come as a surprise to most people, but the solutions seem mostly out of reach. It seems like a problem for the richest of the rich to solve. And in some ways that is true. According to the Credit Suisse Global Wealth Report, the richest 1% holds 43% of all personal wealth.† If you happen to be one of those people, I hope your work is fun, too, but I mainly hope you are actively working toward a better future.

All this is to say we do not need to work more. We do not need to be more productive. Together we need to be better people.

I believe our work is the place where we can do the most good for the world. And I believe we do the best work when we are enthusiastic about it.

---

* "HUD Archives: HUD Releases 2020 Annual Homeless Assessment Report Part 1," March 18, 2021, archives.hud.gov/news/2021/pr21-041.cfm.

† "Top 1 Percent of Households Own 43 Percent of Global Wealth," TRT World, December 7, 2020, www.trtworld.com/magazine/top-1-percent-of -households-own-43-percent-of-global-wealth-42134.

Even if your job is not directly associated with moving humanity forward, a positive spirit will lead to more good going out into the world.

My first five years at King of Pops were the hardest I've ever worked. My comparatively lazy 40-year-old self would politely forgo the opportunity to do it all over again if I knew just how hard it was going to be. It pains me to say it, but those first five years were too hard to willingly opt in to if I knew what I was signing up for.

At the same time, I was having more fun than I'd ever had before. Work had transitioned from the thing I had to do to the thing I wanted to be doing.

I worked late into the night and through the weekends because I was having fun.

I now have a small family and try my very best to head home at 5:30 PM. On walks with my kid, my route almost always swings by King of Pops so I can say hi and check on things. But I work a fraction of the hours I used to.

We go through seasons in our life, but work never has to feel like it's dragging you down.

I admire and relate to the startup founder who is grinding out one-hundred-hour workweeks and never takes vacation to make our world a better place.

And I admire the parents who forgo work completely to stay at home to raise their family, making the world a better place by injecting enthusiasm into their kids.

Despite the thoughts already shared in this book, most people will only work because they have to. It's A-OK if that is the case for you, but just because it's something you have to do doesn't mean you can't enjoy it.

You've got this flicker of light that is your life, and you make the world a better place when you're out having fun in it. Until retirement, if that continues to be a thing, everyone's work should contribute to that better world.

STUMBLING ONTO A PURPOSE

In 2014, we did not have the best benefits package at King of Pops. We squirreled away as much money as possible in order to survive the winter, and we were not yet at a place financially to contribute to the overall health of our team members in some of the traditional ways.

Still, we got creative. We traded pops with restaurants and got everyone together for family meals regularly. We gave out big bonuses when we had a great weekend. However, there was one benefit that did more to shape our company than any other to date.

We had an amazing pop slinger who also happened to be an amazing yoga teacher. Her name was Charlie.

We asked her if she'd be willing to teach a yoga class for our team. Our thought was that this would check a health and wellness box for us. She agreed, and every Tuesday, our slowest day of the week, we met and did yoga together.

We held the classes just off a dirt walking path behind our building, and a handful of neighbors who were walking by at that time each week asked if they could join. Charlie was cool with it, so we agreed, and slowly the class began to grow.

By November, the class had grown to about 30 people every Tuesday. With temperatures dropping, we bookmarked it and agreed we'd start the class again in the spring.

The next year something amazing happened: the class quickly swelled from 30 people to three hundred. And then five hundred. At one point we had over eight hundred people doing yoga in a field with Charlie. She used a bullhorn so people could hear her, but most people couldn't hear much. Everyone just kind of observed their neighbors and did what felt right to them.

The mass of people became a semisynchronized unit. There was something magical about moving in unison with such a large group of people.

There would be someone serious about yoga next to a first-timer wearing jeans and using a bath towel for their yoga mat. They'd all just be watching each other, trying to learn something, but mainly we were a community actually doing something together.

Charlie embodies everything that I love most about King of Pops. She is optimistic and enthusiastic, has an irreverent spirit, and tries her best to have fun.

A couple times a year we'd invite everyone who attended the class to our HQ for a free pop. It wasn't much, but we wanted to say thanks to the community for making the event special.

At some point that year, I remember lying in Savasana, the pose most yoga classes end with, which consists of lying on your back with your eyes closed. This pose is the reward for working hard for the last hour.

Charlie's voice would turn from playful and instructive to soothing and mindful.

I remember lying there on that patchy grass field, overflowing with happiness and pride. Our company, King of Pops, was responsible for starting something truly special. The week prior we had sold over 20 thousand pops at Music Midtown, our business had been recognized in *The Economist,* and we had opened our first brick-and-mortar location. However, this moment felt so much more important.

This moment felt selfless and bigger than what I understood work to be all about.

As I lay on the ground with my eyes closed, I could feel myself smiling. It all seemed so clear to me: creating moments like this was our company's purpose. This is the thing we are here to do.

Soon after that day, a group of us got into a room, picked the right words, and made it official. Our company purpose was to create unexpected moments of happiness. While we still host yoga and other community events, most UMOHs come in the form of surprising folks with free pops in fun ways. It could be during a visit to the cancer ward of a children's hospital, the fire station, the bus drivers' annual conference, or a Dungeons & Dragons meetup.

Free pops are great, but more important is publicly recognizing a person or organization. This selfless act creates community connections in new ways. It starts countless positive conversations that wouldn't happen otherwise.

The unintended consequence of putting good out in the world, in our case through giving out free pops, also feels rewarding. The feeling of pride and happiness I had in the grass during Savasana at our yoga events is something I want our team to experience as well.

These UMOHs do not directly solve any of the world's greatest issues, but we believe they are how we can make the biggest impact as an ice pop company. We believe these acts add up over time, and we look forward to a future in which people are not suspiciously looking for a catch when someone does something nice for them.

SO WHAT DO YOU DO?

Over the last 15 years, people have excitedly walked up to me to ask about King of Pops. As we talk about the company, they say things like "You must be having so much fun" and "You are so lucky."

After going through my King of Pops spiel, I politely return the favor and ask them about their work. Far too often, they begin to squirm. It is difficult to coax more than a sentence or two out of these folks. The Pew Research Center cites that about half of the workforce enjoys their jobs, but in my experience, even fewer people seem to want to talk about it.[*]

These awkward encounters prompted me to write this book.

As you've gathered, I passionately believe work can be fun. I also think work *should* be fun. And I think that when it is fun, we're more likely to move the world forward, solve big problems, and make the world a better place.

Still, I know there will be plenty of objections to why the idea of fun at work "doesn't apply to me."

---

[*] Juliana Menasce Horowitz and Kim Parker, "How Americans View Their Jobs," Pew Research Center, March 20, 2023, www.pewresearch.org /social-trends/2023/03/30/how-americans-view-their-jobs/.

Here are a few of the most common objections and some thoughts to consider if you still find yourself having similar reservations after reading to this point.

"My job is boring."

I worked at the dining hall in college.

I got paid a low hourly rate but was able to eat for as long as I wanted before and after my shift, which made it worthwhile for me.

There was a large staff, and after getting trained, I noticed it was pretty easy to slip into a nonwork abyss and just skate through the shift doing very little. There was a group of employees doing just that every day, and there was another group of employees who were essentially making everything happen.

Early on, I dabbled in both groups.

I probably should have felt guilty for the work-avoidance techniques I tried out, but I didn't at the time. Surprisingly, I willingly joined the group that was working as effectively as they possibly could. This was not a result of a strong moral compass. It just made the time pass faster.

When I was working on the omelet station, mastering my egg flips and suggesting ingredient combinations to the guests, the time flew by.

Conversely, if I took the easy way out, grabbed a spray bottle and a rag and pretended like I was cleaning tables, the time dragged.

I learned every job there, from dishes to salad prep to the grill to the sub sandwich line. It was never boring. Boredom is a choice.

A cross-country drive can be excruciatingly boring for a four-year-old, and the trip of a lifetime for the old-timer who has spent the last few years planning for it. Looking out the window at expansive landscapes can feel blah or offer a world of wonder.

In order for your work to be fun, you have to get curious about it.

Are you doing what you can to make it not boring? Are you asking thoughtful questions and challenging yourself to make things better? Have you done your part to make it fun?

Can you explain exactly what your business does and why they do it?

If you can't, act like an annoying toddler and say "Why?" to your boss over and over until it makes sense.

Once you've done this, your work will almost certainly become more interesting.

"Mixing fun and work dilutes professionalism."

When I met my now wife for the first time, we were at a mutual friend's birthday party. We spent most of that first evening together talking about a fungal outbreak in Mexico. She was working at the Centers for Disease Control and Prevention. I was amazed not only by her beauty but by how passionate she was about something that seemed so prescriptive.

I'm not particularly proud of it, but when I couldn't stop thinking about her, I asked a mutual friend how we could get in touch. She gave me her email, and I sent a message asking if I could take her out for dinner to talk more about what was going on in the fungal public health world.

Pretty romantic, huh?

We have spent the last decade talking a lot about work, and I now get it. Her job is never done; it is a huge challenge, and there are big-time consequences for the work she does. Most importantly, her work very clearly helps people.

You might think the serious nature of her work would translate to a rigid work culture, but that isn't the case. Her branch is a fun bunch that has mushroom-adorned everything.

They have mushroom-inspired shirts that read "I'm a Fungi," and my wife's favorite mug was custom-made and says "I'm a Fun gal." Her boss, Tom, has the inside of his suit jacket adorned with a bright mushroom pattern.

Within the CDC, they are a very small branch, but their quirky culture attracts talent from across the globe, and they can accomplish a lot with a small team because they love what they do.

The no-fun facade that certain job types have created comes from a place of insecurity and misinformation. The people who are the very best in the world at their work have the ability to make it enjoyable for themselves and for everyone around them. They invite people in and could talk at great length about why the work they are doing is important.

Professionalism be damned. Life is short, and it should be enjoyed.

"Focus on fun could overshadow focus on results or key performance indicators."

There is a path where long hours and laser-focus on results is highly productive. The problem is that the path is not healthy to sustain over the long run. A never-ending sprint with no breaks is not pro-ductive if you get burnt out and can't keep it up.

For sustained results, fun needs to be incorporated. In addi-tion, fun helps dramatically when you are trying to get more peo-ple bought into your vision to help achieve a specific result.

"Financial constraints could make fun initiatives seem wasteful."

One of our most fun employees, Tyler Rogers, created a game called Double Deuce that he was convinced could be turned into an on-the-shelf game to be sold at Target if only he got it in front of the right people. I've gotta say, it was pretty darn fun.

The premise was very simple. A group of three or more people would form a circle (the more people, the better). Two different people would start with a ball and toss it to anyone in the circle. If you tried to catch the ball and failed, you were out. If two peo-ple threw the ball to you at the same time and you caught both of them, both throwers were out. Catching two balls at once was called Double Deuce.

Who knows why, but this game stuck.

Tyler seemed to carry these balls everywhere with him. He had a Double Deuce addiction. After meetings, at any extracurricular event, on a random Thursday, he was always itching to play a game. The funny thing was, he wasn't really that interested in winning. He was more of a teacher, moderator, and hype man.

The game became beloved by the entire company during those years. We were writing our 15-year vision for the company at that time, and a reference to the game made it in.

Eventually Tyler moved to Boston with his wife but graciously left two balls, worth about a dollar each, for us to continue playing without him.

Sadly, Double Deuce died when he left. It turned out that it wasn't the game itself that was so much fun. It was Tyler.

It is important to note that fun doesn't need to cost anything. In fact, the most fun usually costs nothing. It comes down to enthusiasm and perspective.

To create a fun work environment, first focus on creating an openness for fun, then fill it with things you can afford. There is nothing worse than feeling a lot of pressure to have fun at an event your company cannot afford.

Build the practice of fun into your DNA instead of trying to create a handful of grandiose events.

"What is fun for one person may not be for the next person. It might even make them uncomfortable."

At King of Pops, we have a volunteer event planning committee.

Larger companies may have a designated role to develop this type of thing, but in smaller companies, the planning and execution of extracurricular events requires a group effort.

We run the event-planning meetings like any other meeting— we progress through an agenda, discuss issues, and assign to-do items. Being part of the committee is optional and takes a backseat to your primary responsibilities. If you agree to do something and your time availability changes, you let the team know, and things are redistributed across the volunteers.

The important part is that we put something on the schedule.

We usually host a handful of planned events each year, and the seed of the idea typically comes from the discussions in those meetings. Because there is a diverse group of employees at the table to discuss the activities, we feel confident that the event will not offend people or be exclusive. It is important to take this step seriously, perhaps even explicitly adding the question, "Will this event hurt anyone's feelings?" as a required discussion topic.

We don't do that, but this intention lives within our "be thoughtful" core value.

Good intentions and a diversity of perspectives in the planning committee do not guarantee that feelings will not get hurt.

For example, our events often have alcohol available. We have team members who are under 21 and others who just don't drink. Ideally, someone in the planning committee falls into this bucket. They would then suggest some nonalcoholic alternatives that we could provide.

Sometimes in our haste, we fail at this one. The options end up being cheap beer and water.

While there is always a risk of what one person finds fun making someone else feel uncomfortable, if different perspectives are attempted to be considered and positive intentions are clear, then having fun at work is well worth the risk.

Certainly, if anyone does not feel comfortable with something happening at work, they should feel empowered to opt out and comfortable to communicate why they don't think a certain activity should be part of a work-sponsored event.

Use your common sense, but trying to create fun should not be scary. If you have positive intentions, push forward, and if you get feedback, receive it as feedback and adjust.

"Fun initiatives could be seen as superficial or gimmicky."

Luckily, fun at King of Pops is in many ways built into the business. We are typically attending events that are already going to be fun, and our little pop cart is an added bonus. For that reason, early on, when the entire company was only a handful of employees, our default team-building would be at the events we were working. At the most-fun events, every once in a while, we'd naturally gather at a single cart and sling pops together. If we were feeling like the day was already a success, or we had sold out of pops, we might pack up a little early to watch the encore at a music festival together before heading home.

During this time, I don't think fun was lacking, because everything was so new.

Even so, I do remember an attempt to do something special. I'm not a cigar smoker. In fact, I don't think any of us had smoked a full cigar at that point in our lives. They kind of make me sick, but there was a cigar lounge a block or so away from our pop kitchen, and the owner invited us down.

So the four of us, the entire company at the time, decided to host a planning meeting there. With cigars slowly simmering, we talked about what the rest of the season and what the next few years should look like. We lit cigars and reclined obnoxiously far back into the large leather chairs. We celebrated wins and toasted each other excessively.

The change of scenery was silly and unnecessary but made the meeting fun and memorable.

My point is that an activity can be superficial and gimmicky, and it can be fun. They are not mutually exclusive. It isn't worth overthinking because each person will have a different view on this. The important thing is to do something.

As soon as you start trying to be cool, you will not be cool. Like anything, the more you do it, the better you get at it. The more frequently you attempt fun, the less you'll end up at an event that is supposed to be fun but is just awkward instead.

"Employees might abuse 'fun' policies, like unlimited PTO or relaxed dress codes."

In my experience, they just don't.

In fact, we've found you need to encourage folks to do the behaviors that protect them from their "work is supposed to be hard" tendencies.

For most of our salaried staff, we have an unlimited PTO policy, but in reality, leadership sets the tone. A policy is a framework that helps the employee know what the expectation is. They are important but usually are only referenced when there is a problem.

Employees really end up copying the patterns they see around them. This is why a great culture is so much more important than a great employee handbook.

As you know by now, I enjoy working. So for years it seemed like I was taking zero vacations other than our company-mandated "surf break" (for our first decade, we closed completely for two weeks in the winter). I eventually realized people were mirroring the behaviors that Nick and I were presenting, which was a "work all the time" mentality. Typically, we weren't working all the time because we had to but because we wanted to.

We'd visit a customer down the street from the lake we were visiting with the family, pop in for a virtual meeting after we hit the slopes for the day, or respond to emails in the morning before heading to the beach.

It didn't feel like work to us, but it set the precedent that this was the expectation for our team. People learn the culture by seeing it firsthand, and while our PTO policy was generous, our culture around it was not.

A number of studies reinforce the mixed messages sent by an unlimited PTO policy. The Society for Human Relations Managers found that many employees with unlimited days off take far less than the two weeks most employers offer.* The days of the unlimited PTO policy seeming like a uniquely great benefit are over.

Still, at our company, it works well most of the time. In general, people take two to four weeks off. It works for us because it sets the precedent of trust.

When done right, it allows for the employee to weigh the pros and cons of taking a vacation at a specific time. If we are trusting them to manage a huge budget, it makes sense to apply this same level of trust to the other parts of their work life, right?

Within our companies, we have a lot of unique business challenges. Instead of trying to design and continually update a policy that works for our complex needs, we trust the team to do it for themselves.

---

* Joanne Sammer, "4 Lessons About Unlimited Vacation," Society for Human Relations Managers, January 6, 2020, www.shrm.org/topics-tools /news/benefits-compensation/4-lessons-unlimited-vacation.

We generate most of our revenue between April and October. Our operations team has to work very hard to make this happen. At the same time, if our accountant wants to take a week off during an operationally hectic week, it isn't a big deal. If our bar manager wants to take a couple weeks off in peak season, it is going to have a major impact on the success of the business. We've found that they understand this without much explanation. At the same time, they should know that if the manager's sister is getting married in Fiji, they obviously need to go.

For work to be sustainable and productive, it needs to be built on trust. Trust is a key ingredient in making your work fun.

As you design policies, it is easy to think of the edge cases and ways that people could take advantage of the situation. The sweet spot is to create a set of policies that provide clarity for a new employee from their first day but don't hamstring freedom for the people having fun at work and creating value for the organization.

"Trying to make work fun might inadvertently lead to more stress to maintain that atmosphere."

Every year in November, we wrap up the pop season with a thank-you party to the community for another year of support. We call it King of Pops Field Day.

We give away free pops and have music, food trucks, and lots of games.

Every year we'll have some random attraction like an ice carving, pop bingo, or fire dancers. Puddles Pity Party used to be a recurring guest, but he's too popular these days.

We've done sack races and dunk booths (risky in late fall). For a few years, we held pop-eating contests, but we stopped doing that for fear we'd get sued.

The main event is the games. You'll get some game tickets when you arrive, and you can win prize tickets for King of Pops merch and other little toys.

Some examples of our more cavalier games are bush toss, where you try to toss a ball into a bush and get it to stop in certain areas. Beat the pro in Ping-Pong—last year I was the pro, and all you have to do is win a game to five. But most of them are DIY knockoffs of carnival classics like can pyramid knockdown, ring toss, and bucket toss.

The event checks a number of boxes:

- It's an opportunity to engage with our most loyal customers.
- It helps us get rid of some inventory before the winter.
- It's a chance to promote our other businesses (Perfect 10 Foods, King of Crops, RainbowProvisions.com).
- And most importantly, it's an honest attempt to have fun with the team.

It requires a lot of volunteers to operate the games. And for the games to be any fun, the volunteers must be having fun: challenging, prodding, teasing, and ultimately celebrating with the guests as they get ultracompetitive in an attempt to win prize tickets that are only worth a couple of bucks.

I'm the type of person who starts to stress big-time the day of the event. I convince myself that nobody is going to show up. Every time, without fail, I'm happy midway through the day.

The volunteer team gets free drinks, food, shirts, and a big thank-you.

I always dread setting it up. And then I'm always glad we did it.

Hosting fun activities can certainly seem like a waste of time and just one more thing to do, but if you value it, you'll see the benefits.

"Not all jobs can be made 'fun.' Think about critical or high-stress roles."

At King of Pops, believe it or not, we have some pretty high-stress moments.

Delta Airlines is one of our best customers, and nearly every year they treat their team to pops. The events have grown over the years, and in 2023 the cost of the activation had grown to $40,000 to treat their team (10 thousand-plus people) to pops for the day. We had to get background checks, license plate verifications, and special clearance to drive next to the runways. We spent the day before packing up the order into 20 carts and every cooler we could find so we could efficiently execute on the big day.

After coordinating details for months, we always ended up super stressed the morning of the event. Trucks don't work, umbrellas get lost, people show up late.

In these moments, we remind ourselves: "At the end of the day, the worst thing that can happen is someone is not going to get a pop."

While that is less than ideal, the stakes are not that high. Usually, in the same breath, we say something like "We aren't doing brain surgery."

But what if you are a brain surgeon? I don't think that means you should have to abstain from fun at work.

To be clear, most of the fun outlined in this book is A-OK for any job type at any time. Pride, ownership, patience, story, and perspective are all helpful in even the most high-stress environments. Play, on the other hand, has a place and time.

I know I would not want a dentist to wield a drill without their full attention on the job at hand.

This is true for most work. There are times when play is not appropriate. We just shouldn't let the needs of the highest-stress moments of a job dictate the rest of the time working.

Surgeons spend time outside of surgery.

Lawyers spend time outside the courtroom.

First responders spend time waiting to respond.

In all work there is downtime. This is the time to inject a bit of play. Not only does it make life more enjoyable, it helps us do our jobs better when the high-stress moments inevitably arrive.

"Having fun at work could make it harder to disconnect and establish work-life boundaries."

My wife and I have a relatively new practice of forcing ourselves to sit down and talk through our schedules together. We have a small whiteboard taped to the back of the door of our coat closet, and once a month, we stare at it and try to figure out how to make all of the pieces fit together.

There is more work, family, and social stuff than we can fit. And together we decide what makes the most sense.

I was 31 and she was 29 when we met. At that point we had both spent the last decade living life day to day. Before we met, we were both laser-focused on our career goals, and even after we met, our life outside of work mostly just filled in around the edges when work was not present.

We laugh to ourselves when we think of the days when we would be driving by the movie theater and decide on a whim to pull in and watch something. With a young family, we are now doing good if we remember all the teacher workdays and seemingly random dates when preschool is closed. We are constantly navigating the labyrinth of our work schedules, childcare schedule, volunteer days, and hopefully a few dates together.

In the movie-theater-on-a-whim phase, it would not be strange for one of us to unexpectedly stay at work for a couple extra hours, leaving the other to fend for themselves for dinner.

Now everything is scheduled. A normal workweek allows me to get started on Monday, Wednesday, and Friday by 9:15 AM. On those days, I strap my two-year-old on my bike, drop her off at preschool at 8:55 AM, the earliest allowed, and race to work. On Tuesday and Thursday, I hit the interstate to take her to her grandma's house about 20 miles away, then roll the dice with traffic, hoping I'll make it back in time for my first meeting of the day.

A normal day allows me to focus on work from the moment I arrive until five o'clock. Time flies when you're having fun, and I rarely get everything done that I'd like to. At five, I look at what I'm doing and check in with myself to make sure it is something that is adding value. If it is, I will allow myself to keep working on it, with a self-imposed deadline of 5:30 PM.

I'm responsible for the mornings and getting everyone to school, and my wife gets started and ends her day earlier to manage the first part of the evening. However, if I stay any later than 5:30 PM, I feel like I'm missing out on what's happening at home.

My point in sharing all this: just because something is fun doesn't mean you should be doing it all the time. In my twenties, when work hours felt like an unlimited resource, I was having a lot of fun at work, but honestly, it feels like I'm having more fun working now that it is a set piece of time that I have to look forward to.

In the evening and on my days off, I do my best to resist checking my email to see if there have been any updates. Then when everyone goes to bed, I usually take a moment to check in on things before I call it a night. Not because I have to but because I want to.

Writing out a "whole life" schedule is a great way to make sure the boxes that matter most to you in life are being checked. Our coat closet whiteboard doesn't get referenced that often, but the exercise of filling it out together is a process that helps put things in perspective.

Activating other parts of your life will only enhance your appreciation of the time when you do work. *Work Is Fun* is the title of this book, but the real goal is for life to be fun. When we find balance, we are able to better appreciate the variety of challenges and experiences that we have.

"Companies may use 'fun' as an excuse not to pay workers more."

In the early days of King of Pops, our salaries were not as high as we would have liked.

The pop season is relatively short, and our revenue wasn't very stable. Without any outside funding, it would have been irresponsible to commit to paying folks more than we knew we could afford.

However, we found ways to make the jobs appealing. Since the winter was already going to be slow, we implemented a surf break, in which we closed for a month to rest and recharge our batteries. People could work cross-functionally, so our accountants would have the opportunity to work a music festival or vend at the Super Bowl. And there was always a new pop flavor being passed around to weigh in on.

These days our compensation has caught up. We pay at or above market rates and offer a profit share that everyone participates in, and the free pops are still flowing.

These compensation strategies are different, but one is not better than the other.

At the end of the day, a company is going to pay what it feels like it can afford. More sophisticated large corporations know that if their labor margin is too low, they may be profitable in the short term, but that could be at the cost of innovation and larger gains in the future.

I'm convinced that these two things, fun at work and compensation, are not as correlated as many people think. It is fun to receive a large paycheck, but it is more fun to be doing work that is meaningful to you.

What is fun and meaningful for one person may not be fun for another.

Ultimately, it is up to the individual to decide if a job is the right one for them. We can hope that a company will create a fun work environment, but it takes two to tango, and the individual worker is just as important to the equation as the company.

CONCLUSION
Making Work Fun Takes Work . . .
But It's Worth It

What does the future of work hold?

When we don't solve for fun at work, here is the best-case scenario from my perspective:

The world comes together and lands on a generous universal basic income. Without any unintended consequences, robots and AI gleefully execute all the necessities that we've been begrudgingly doing for thousands of years.

This efficiency allows everyone to get paid more, and the new norm is a three-day workweek, giving us more time than ever to be with our family and pursue our hobbies.

I'm an optimist, but even I don't think this future will happen.

Still, let's just say it did.

What would really change?

Would your 10% bigger house feel any different, especially if everyone else's house got 10% bigger as well?

Would flushing 20 hours of work instead of 40 down the toilet feel that much different after the newness had worn off?

I don't think so.

As long as there is work, there is a strong case to improve it.

"Love what you do, and you'll never work a day in your life," a quote attributed to many, is so true and also not so useful on the surface. When we are anxiously fretting about our career, first entering the workforce, finishing up college, or experiencing a mid-life crisis, quotes like these bang around in our head incessantly.

The idea of loving what you do led me to Idaho to write about sports. Because I wasn't talented enough to get paid to play sports, I figured writing about them was the next best thing. I was unhappy with that job because I was hoping I would show up and everything would fall into place. I hoped to love it right away in a way that I was familiar with.

When that didn't happen quickly, I gave up on the whole "love what you do" thing and settled for a higher salary instead.

Looking back, I wasn't looking for love correctly. The quote has circulated so widely and consistently because it is spot-on about loving what you do, but we gloss over the fact that love itself is hard work.

When we think about romantic love, we are willing to put in hard work. It's a commitment, and when we get married, we vow to be patient, communicate, and compromise. As our lives get busy, we schedule date nights to make sure we're having fun together. Romantic love isn't easy, but most agree it's worth the effort.

If you modify that quote with these ideas in mind, it doesn't roll off the tongue quite the same way, but the idea becomes significantly more useful.

Maybe it should be revised to say: "Work hard, be patient, communicate, and have fun at what you do, and you won't work a day in your life."

I've found this to be the case.

It seems to me that most of the concepts we consider to be true when looking for romantic love are good metaphors for our quest for fun at work:

- If someone is attractive, this doesn't mean they'll be a great partner.

    Sad but true. You can dress a job up with amazing perks, a beautiful office, and a relaxed atmosphere, but once the newness wears off, the underlying work will still be there. That underlying work is what needs to become fun to you.

- Marrying for money usually doesn't end well.

    Money certainly allows for happiness. It can make a lot of things in life easier, but it does not lead to happiness on its own. In much the same way, our salary will not lead to long-term fulfillment.

- Sharing a hobby or interest is nice but not necessary.

    When you are first getting to know someone, it is super helpful to have a shared interest so you can get to know them, but over time this shared interest matters less and less. The big stuff is happening everywhere else. The same is true at work; we will not automatically love working on something just because at one point we did it for fun.

As a society we've mostly come around to the idea that our relationship with our significant other will take a great deal of hard work to maintain. We might not always want to do the hard work, but we have a sense that it is worth it in the long run.

I hate to admit that that whole "happy wife, happy life" thing has some wisdom to it.

We need to reframe our quest for fun at work with a similar spirit. Just as we can't find true love overnight, we won't fall in love with our job on day one.

If I could give my college-age self some career advice, I would urge him to spend a lot less time thinking about what career path will pay the most, be the easiest, or make him feel the coolest.

I'd urge him to be patient, and instead of jumping into action, to sit quietly with his own thoughts and try to understand what he is good at doing, and what problems in the world he feels most drawn to helping solve.

These questions aren't any easier, but they set the stage for work to be meaningful and fun.

I'm happy to report that I love my job, but I was lucky to end up where I am today. I'm well suited for small business because I am able to motivate a team and I'm a generalist: pretty good at a lot of things but truly great at nothing.

When it comes to a problem in the world, it took us a while to unlock what was right in front of us—our company purpose to create unexpected moments of happiness. The problem we're solving is the lack of kindness in the world. I've adopted that as my own.

It would have been really tough to proactively land on the parts of my work that seem so clear to me today. It took a false start in journalism, an insurance job that I was doing for all the wrong reasons, and the Great Recession to take me where I was supposed to be.

Steve Jobs has a great quote, delivered during his 2005 commencement address at Stanford, that helps me to find comfort in the uncertainty we inevitably find ourselves in during our careers:

> "You can't connect the dots looking forward; you can only connect them looking backward. So you have to trust that the dots will somehow connect in your future. You have to trust in something—your gut, destiny, life, karma, whatever. This approach has never let me down, and it has made all the difference in my life."

Every step along the way is part of the path to where you are supposed to go, so you might as well enjoy it.

Each of us holds our own key to our very best future of work. And as fanciful as it might sound, that key really is having fun.

There is no downside to this future for anyone.

We live in a world of polarizing topics, but having fun at work is not one.

I believe we are at the very beginning of a movement to create fun, meaningful workplaces. Right now a company prioritizing fun at work is an anomaly, but in the future, this will become more of an expectation.

For decades, car salespeople had a huge advantage over the customer. They were relied upon as the source of information for the product they were selling. Information is power, and they were able to manipulate the customer in order to achieve their goals.

Today companies like Tesla and Carvana sell most of their cars through their website, bypassing car dealers completely. If you go to a car lot to buy a car today, the salesperson is looked at as a nuisance, not a resource.

The data to make an informed decision is readily available online, and we're each empowered to go out and get it. Be wary of the promises in job postings. Seek out feedback from people who have worked there in the past and continue to work there today.

We use the internet in this way for most of our major life decisions but not nearly as effectively when it comes to our work.

Glassdoor, LinkedIn, and Indeed masquerade as information hubs. They are good resources, but they are still job boards at their cores. Media outlets publish various "best place to work" reports, but companies often have to pay to be considered, leaving many of the actual best places to work on the sideline.

While some information online is helpful, it is mostly ignored. When a job offer is received, people's attention darts to salary, benefits, and where they are able to work.

In general, large companies provide better benefits and are more stable, while small companies are more flexible and offer a closer-knit community.

Both have the capacity to be fun, but this ends up being an area that is left out of the job postings because we lack constructive words to talk about it.

If you're looking for a job at a large company, this information is often available, and more and more people are going to prioritize fun when deciding where they work. When the information is not available, it is worth it to ask tough questions to the hiring manager and request to contact former employees to ask about their experiences. In much the same way employers do reference checks, you should reach out to former employees to get a true sense of the culture.

If you are in the interview process and they ask you if you have any questions, ask, "What is your favorite part about working here?"

When it comes to employers prioritizing fun at work, we are at the beginning of the bell curve. Early adopters are awkwardly figuring out how to fit fun into the workday that has always prioritized day-to-day productivity. But as our world gets more connected, these early adopters will get an outsized amount of attention.

At some point, though, I hope fun at work will be expected. Companies will fight to find ways to make their employees' lives more meaningful. And employees looking to have fun will further amplify the missions they are aligned with.

Although I'm an optimist, I'm also a realist.

I know there are companies that will continue to disregard fun at work, and just like bad actors have persisted and found success for so long, these "unfun" workplaces will continue to exist.

Reality is disappointing in that way.

But the good news is, you can make your own choice to have fun at work or seek a workplace where you can.

The very act of trying to have fun at work is a win-win. It's good for the company, and it's good for you.

Finding your fun is ultimately your responsibility. In most cases, you'll be able to find it regardless of your setting, but if you've done the work outlined in this book and something about your current environment is holding you back, it's time to move on.

You can have fun at work, and you deserve it.

Having fun at work is 100% something you deserve to do for yourself. And at the same time, the more of us that are having fun, the better off the world will be.

Our time on earth is tragically short. You cannot afford to waste a moment.

Go have some fun.

OUR 2030 VISION STATEMENT

This vision was written in 2015, and although so much has changed in our business, it helps guide us 10 years later.

To those who refuse to just exist,

In 2010, we didn't start with a formal business plan. There wasn't a focus group that selected the rainbow umbrella that now casts shade over hundreds of pushcarts throughout the South. Our professional culinary experience was nonexistent.

So how did we get here? The reality is that I was 25 and the idea of selling pops for the summer seemed like fun. We chose the first rainbow umbrella because it was in stock and we could afford it. As for making pops, well, we just hoped we could figure that out.

The idea of what exists today was not imaginable. Yet years later, the stories of our success are retold like folklore. Looking back, it's easy to gloss over the details that propelled us to where we are today. I wouldn't trade that journey for anything.

Our origins are pretty well documented. Nick and I would work through the night to make pops and wake up early the next morning to sell them. We jumped at any opportunity that came our way, and the money started to add up. Eventually we started to have a real business. We had to laugh at how lucky we were.

However, what Nick and I started was only the beginning of what we have now. The "secret," our single greatest achievement, has been inspiring a group of employees who connect with what is going on. What started as a job for so many is now so much more. Our constant sacrifice is draining and exhilarating at the same time.

If you choose to work here, I hope you feel that you are a part of something great, a project more important and worthwhile than something any one of us could accomplish on our own—that your time, the most precious thing we have, is being spent wisely.

Important change is happening here right now. Don't let it get lost in the day-to-day—I'm 100% confident that it is happening.

Let's never stop pushing each other. These are the good ol' days. Here is a glance at what we all have to look forward to in 2030. A sincere thank-you to everyone who helped make this a reality.

—Steve Carse

This vision verbalizes our core values and begins to establish why we operate.

✦ *Be Thoughtful* ✦ *Get Sweaty* ✦ *Good Vibes Only* ✦
✦ *Wear the Shirt* ✦ *Stay Hungry* ✦ *Get It Done* ✦

RAINBOW UMBRELLA 2030 VISION

Our Neighbors Smile When They See Us

Every year, we've started and ended the season with some type of thank-you to our community. Typically it includes free pops and a handful of other ideas that seem fun, silly, or strange in the moment. The simple gesture goes a long way in explaining how and why we operate.

If we can consistently sweeten the lives of our neighbors and enjoy doing it, we all win.

This year is special. Our 20th year has come to a close, and the similarities to the early days outnumber the differences. We still host a party, the informal nature is still endearing, and we are still giving away pops to anyone who will have one.

What started as a King of Pops celebration now incorporates bits and pieces from each brand under the Rainbow Umbrella. Attendance is optional, but employees new and old rarely miss the occasion. A group that has never met has an immediate bond, laughing and comparing stories about what has changed and what is still the same. Most importantly, they talk excitedly about what is to come.

The same enthusiasm permeates our organization every day. Significant others and friends have gotten used to hearing work talk hours after we've officially "clocked out" for the day. It's not always our fault—if you're within a couple blocks of HQ and you happen to be wearing a company T-shirt, it's pretty common for a stranger to walk up and start a conversation about the latest project.

It's nice to be loved, and our response is to love back. We like to have fun, and for us it's more fun when we invite our neighbors. We're active in the community far beyond our business, whether it's a huge event like Field Day (which is essentially just a staff party that we decided to invite the city to), the annual field trips that dozens of inner-city schools take to a King of Crops outpost, the latest community service project that was conceived by our Do-Gooder committee, or any of the hundreds of new, half-baked ideas we try each year that make just enough sense to work.

Our Front Porch

Our umbrella covers the South, from Richmond to Orlando and New Orleans to Charleston. We have nearly a dozen hubs in the largest markets, and outposts scattered in between. Each city is unique, but the positive vibe is consistent.

If you leave work for the day as others are winding down, you'll probably see a group of employees hanging out together. Perhaps just having a beer, or maybe playing a new game with ever-evolving rules. On out-of-town trips, an informal visit to other Rainbow Umbrella spots is an activity usually on the schedule.

There is a natural tension between our desire to grow and our belief that our impact is diminished if we spread too far geographically. Focusing on the South allows us to remain an important influence in the local food scene. It puts us in a position to have authentic relationships with our neighbors. It's why half our customers have been to one of our farms at some point—to pull a weed, attend a wedding ceremony, or just enjoy the scenery.

That's something global brands cannot compete with.

The South is not a geographic area that we've identified as an ideal place to operate a business. It's our home and the place where we want to see and effect change.

Employee Partners

Most of our hubs started out as King of Pops kitchens, but it's astounding to see the variety of businesses that have evolved from selling ice pops. One of the first was Perfect 10 Foods, a local food distribution company, which started when we realized we had extra space on our trucks during wholesale deliveries and knew a group of friends who were trying to get their own amazing products in front of a similar audience. Eventually it became an incredibly successful autonomous business, and while it could easily justify its own facility, we work right next to each other because the unexpected organic interactions are where the magic happens.

We are an open and inclusive group that values and seeks out different perspectives. We constantly learn from each other, bring in experts to expand our minds to new ideas, and have a first-class training program that all employees must complete. This quest to learn and teach was fully realized when we chose to open our doors to the world and started a self-growth and business training spinoff. Its approachable and fun reputation has attracted students from around the world, and it's where we go to be inspired and reminded why we're here.

Employees act like and are treated like partners because of those that came before them. There are numerous examples of an employee having a great idea, running with it, and changing both their own future and the future of the organization. A new business with a new cofounder is started every couple years.

This mentality is contagious. It's absolutely vital for our employees to have the ability to translate the work they are doing to the bigger picture. They are taught how their business operates, and they understand why decisions at all levels are being made.

We require a commitment that extends beyond the typical nine-to-five business arrangement. It isn't necessarily more hours, but dedication and a sense of pride in your work is a must. Life-work balance is taken seriously, but when an idea strikes at midnight, sometimes we can't help but call our peers to talk about it.

We help each other out and push ourselves to the limit when the situation calls for it. These are the times when coworkers turn into family. We take care of our family. We celebrate Thanksgiving together at each King of Crops outpost, the kids play on soccer teams together, and Steve still offers up his condo to visiting employees when he's on the road.

Financially, everyone knows and is excited by the opportunity to make a good income. A forward-thinking vacation policy, retirement plan, and other outstanding benefits are continuously monitored and improved.

Product Is King

Our product and service strategy couldn't be more straightforward: do your absolute best to create something amazing.

We know we can't do that on our own. We decided early on that it's best to hide nothing. Instead, we bring our customers along for the ride. For better or for worse, we let them in. At King of Pops, that meant going into detail about which pops were great and which could use some work. On our farm, we invite experts out when we are trying something new. At P10, our customers rate every single delivery, and we make changes even if it makes things a little more difficult.

The same folks who started as seasonal kitchen workers several years ago, cutting thousands of strawberries with dull paring knives, still walk the kitchen floor to make sure things are done right. Their eyes light up when the newest improvement is shared, and the communication and respect between new and old employees is both casual and crucial because it allows us to forever improve.

We've learned that by being transparent, vulnerable, and helpful, people will go out of their way to help us succeed. Our products and services are the best of their kind in the world because we keep it simple, care about what we're doing, and never stop finding ways to do it better.

Sustainability: Beyond the Buzzword

To us sustainability always seemed obvious. As we grow, we take our responsibility more seriously and push ourselves to become an example of business doing good.

To the world, what first comes to mind is our commitment to environmental sustainability. It's why we recycle or compost 99% of our waste. It's why at least 90% of our produce is locally or organically sourced. It's why we operate a regional organic farming operation and teach thousands of people every year how to do the same.

Internally, those same ideals are shared, but our focus is on a different type of sustainability. It is highlighted by our insistence on maintaining a healthy business for our Rainbow Umbrella family, creating a stable business that generates enough profit to continually invest in our people and the new ideas they bring to the table.

Our growth has been impressive. We are now a $25 million-per-year business with an 8% profit margin after tax.

We are proud of our humble roots and never consider the temptation of the flashy things that we don't truly need. We drive each truck in our well-maintained fleet for at least a decade instead of wasting money on constant upgrades. We stay at a budget hotel, where we can have just as much fun as if we stayed in the luxury alternative.

There is a big difference between how we function and being cheap. We've proven time and time again that when the situation calls for it, we will spend big. Investment in new ventures and technology are regularly being weighed and planned. We choose to be creative and innovative instead of always using money for an easy fix.

It's financial sustainability, and it's vital for every employee to embrace every day.

Conclusion

From the beginning, people came to King of Pops because it was a little different; not so different that it wasn't accessible but different enough to make a statement and become recognized for it. Putting basil or beets in pops, delivering Christmas trees in elf outfits, growing our own ingredients—there was always a new idea, and we weren't afraid to try it.

Whether or not the ideas come to fruition doesn't matter—we will continue to push each other forward because it's what we want to do.

We're proud of what we do, we're proud of what we make, we're proud of who we work with, we're proud of how we've grown, we're proud of our community, and we're proud that we're still here today to share it with another generation.

It's really pretty simple: love what you do, and that love will be returned tenfold.

ACKNOWLEDGMENTS

Thanks to my mom and dad for the endless support and encouraging me to mix business with pleasure from a very early age.

Thanks to Nancy, Leigh, and Will for creating something I love coming home to.

Thanks to Nick and Ash for being amazing brothers, friends, and co-adventurers.

Thanks to Joe, who helped me organize my thoughts, and Katie for helping me refine them.

And last but not least, thank you to the King of Pops family new and old that have helped me make my work so much fun for so long.

ABOUT THE AUTHOR

 Steve Carse is the co-founder of King of Pops, one of Atlanta's best-loved brands. Steve was named one of *The Atlanta Journal Constitution*'s Most Admired CEOs in 2017 and was included in Georgia Trend's 40 Under 40 list in 2012, but back in 2009, he had just been laid off from his corporate job during the Great Recession and instead of brushing up his resume to work for another company, he decided to start an ice pop business, an idea he and his two brothers, Nick and Ashley, had dreamed up during trips through Central America. Now, King of Pops is the largest cart-based business in the United States, and a $10 million company that sells not just ice pops but Christmas trees, cocktails (aka pop-tails), farm produce, and more.

A dad, hot dog/cotton candy/beer/ice pop slinger, and serial entrepreneur, Steve is always trying his best to slow down, enjoy the ride, and realize that these are the good ol' days.

Want to try a pop? Find one of our carts and have one on us.

Interested in slinging pops for a living? It's a pretty *fun* gig. Visit kingofpops.com to learn more and get started. Mention "Work Is Fun" when you reach out—we'd love to hear from you!